University Life

You may also be interested in the following study titles by Palgrave Macmillan:

14 Days to Exam Success *Lucinda Becker*
Brilliant Writing Tips for Students *Julia Copus*
Cite Them Right (8th edn) *Richard Pears and Graham Shields*
Critical Thinking Skills (2nd edn) *Stella Cottrell*
The Exam Skills Handbook (2nd edn) *Stella Cottrell*
Getting Critical *Kate Williams*
How to Get a First *Michael Tefula*
How to Use Your Reading in Your Essays (2nd edn) *Jeanne Godfrey*
How to Write Better Essays (2nd edn) *Bryan Greetham*
The Palgrave Student Planner *Stella Cottrell*
Planning Your Essay *Janet Godwin*
Reading and Making Notes *Jeanne Godfrey*
Referencing and Understanding Plagiarism *Kate Williams and Jude Carroll*
Reflective Writing *Kate Williams, Mary Woolliams and Jane Spiro*
Report Writing *Michelle Reid*
Skills for Success (2nd edn) *Stella Cottrell*
Studying with Dyslexia *Janet Godwin*
Study Skills Connected *Stella Cottrell and Neil Morris*
The Study Skills Handbook (3rd edn) *Stella Cottrell*
Time Management *Kate Williams and Michelle Reid*
The Undergraduate Research Handbook *Gina Wisker*
Write it Right (2nd edn) *John Peck and Martin Coyle*
Writing for University *Jeanne Godfrey*
You2Uni *Stella Cottrell*

For a complete listing of all titles in our Study Skills range please visit **www.palgrave.com/studyskills**

University Life
Making it Work for You

Lauren Lucien

palgrave
macmillan

© Lauren Lucien 2012

First published 2012 by
PALGRAVE MACMILLAN
Palgrave Macmillan in the UK is an imprint of Macmillan Publishers Limited,
registered in England, company number 785998, of Houndmills,
Basingstoke, *2011001765*
Hampshire RG21 6XS.

Palgrave Macmillan in the US is a division of St Martin's Press LLC,
175 Fifth Avenue, New York, NY 10010.

Palgrave Macmillan is the global academic imprint of the above companies
and has companies and representatives throughout the world.

Palgrave® and Macmillan® are registered trademarks in the United States,
the United Kingdom, Europe and other countries

ISBN: 978-0-230-39231-1

A catalogue record for this book is available from the British Library.

A catalog record for this book is available from the Library of Congress.

10   9   8   7   6   5   4   3   2   1
21 20 19 18 17 16 15 14 13 12

Printed in China

'Finishing is better than starting, patience is better than pride.'

Ecclesiastes 7:8 (New Living Translation)

Contents

About the Author

Lauren Lucien is a Creative Writing with English Literature graduate. She spent the first year of her degree at Blackpool and the Fylde College and the second and third years at Kingston University.

Lauren is a published poet, tutor and academic adviser. In 2011 she was nominated as one of the top 100 African and African-Caribbean graduates and was featured in the *Future Leaders* magazine in partnership with Barclays Capital. This is her first book.

xii

Acknowledgements

Thanks to Liam and Larry for the love and space to write.

Thanks to Karee, Lucy, Harry, Daisy, Becca and Maryam for sharing your 'Inside Stories' with us and also all the friends, family and the many, many students who helped me to complete this book with your tips and advice – couldn't have done it without you all!

Special thanks to Michelle Hayward and Chris Hepworth at Blackpool and the Fylde College, and Siobhan Campbell, Kathryn Maris and Belinda Webb at Kingston University for all their consistent encouragement and belief in me.

Mum for always taking me to the library when I was little and teaching me how to read.

Martha and Max for being the best young writers I know.

Extra special thanks to Suzannah Burywood for taking a chance on me and always being so helpful, forward thinking and encouraging.

Introduction

I remember the day I started writing this book. In the news that week every television channel showed coverage of students from all races, areas and backgrounds, as well as university staff and citizens, protesting over the rise in university tuition fees. In my opinion all students had a right to protest – tuition fees can now be charged up to *triple* the amount they originally were, whereas just over ten years ago they were zero!

One of the reasons I wrote this book is that I also felt and still feel the frustration of a student at having to pay those fees. Now that you are investing so much of your future earnings, make university life work for *you*. This book aims to help you to get more than you expect out of university and to become a successful, optimistic graduate.

First things first, though. I've included a 'University Dictionary' at the end of the book, since if you can speak the lingo it's going to be a whole lot easier to know what to do and how to do it. Getting ready to go can also take some preparation, so I've included some lists to help you. Being a fresher and moving in with new people will be a lifestyle change, but you'll enjoy it and make some good friends along the way if you follow the advice in this book.

Food, money and working at university are all preparation for life after your studies, so see this as a dual-purpose training ground. You may make mistakes and mess things up occasionally, but that's OK, because it's all part of the experience.

Getting the balance right between studying and your new life is part of your learning experience too. You don't know what challenges lie ahead, but there are chapters devoted to helping you through them before they arrive and after they come along.

The final chapter congratulates you. It takes a strong person to make it through to the end and stick with university life. I can say honestly that it will be hard, it will be fun and it will be worth it. I hope this book is helpful and fun to read and that it helps you enjoy your time at university and make the most of it!

How to Use This Book

You don't need to read this book from beginning to end. Take your time over each section and dip in and out whenever you want. I've included some different helpful boxes throughout the book, which I'll explain here.

There are 'intro' and 'outro' boxes that explain the last and next chapter or wrap up the one you're reading.

> So, you've got your finances sorted, you're in your new pad, everything's unpacked (on the floor) and you're ready to get started at uni! This chapter covers all you need to know about Freshers' Week and, more importantly, how to get a headstart on your new life.

There are 'Inside tip' boxes, which contain tips from other students that help and give different points of view.

> ### 💬 Inside tip
>
> 'I went to lectures but skipped quite a few seminars because I thought they were less important – big mistake. I missed out on sharing my work with everyone else and didn't get the feedback I needed to help me make it better. If I could change anything about my first year it would be not skipping classes.'
>
> *Jon, 28, Bristol*

Other boxes are filled with 'Need to know' information.
Books, websites and other helpful media are included here.

> ### ⓘ Need to know...
> If you want more help with avoiding plagiarism, the
> book to get hold of is *Referencing and Understanding
> Plagiarism* by Kate Williams and Jude Carroll. It's a small,
> handy-sized book from the Palgrave Macmillan Pocket
> Study Skills series. Someone gave me a copy and I use it
> alongside my assignments. Keep it inside your bag so it's
> available when you need it.

There are also boxes for generating money by making your university
life work for you, literally. In the age where tuition fees have tripled it's
important to realise that you can make money from your experience
while you are still at university.

> ### ☺ Pocket money generator
> Can you use your experience as a fresher to become a
> freshers' welcomer at your uni next year? Relive Freshers'
> Week and earn a few bob? Sounds good to me!

Lastly, there are sections of the book called 'The Inside Story', where a
student has shared their honest experience of university life and how
they made it work for them. I include some of my own stories here too.

Getting Ready to Go

So, you've been accepted, you have your enrolment dates and you're all packed up and ready to go. All except for those first-night noodles and your duvet cover, oh and your DVD box set of *24* and... well, you get the point!

This chapter is devoted to helping you get everything together, get settled in and get ready to start the craziness that is Freshers' Week.

Savvy?

'Savvy' is probably a word you've heard Captain Jack Sparrow mention a few times, but in this chapter it means being wise with your finances.

Setting yourself up for university can be expensive, so to save on spending, ask your family if they have spare towels, pots and pans and other things like that for you to take with you. Also, there isn't a certain 'brand' that you have to use at university, and it's a lot less scary when you have stuff in your new room that you're familiar with.

You can probably nab most of your packing list from your own home, but check out pound shops for any extras. Bigger shops like IKEA are great for cheap furnishings and accessories, but it's best to keep the budget low when you start out. You'll need extra money in the first few months for having fun and socialising. When you get your student loan or wages you can upgrade the things you need if you want. Of course, if you do have spare money for furnishing your new space then go for it – just remember that student rooms get a lot more wear and tear than your average bedroom at home, so buy things that you don't mind getting knocked or used a lot.

But, before you end up with a car piled high with a mountain of pans, duvets, clothes and the odd teddy hanging on for dear life, have a look at the university packing list I've made below.

The ultimate packing list

Official stuff – best kept in a concertina document folder

☐ Driving licence, both parts

☐ Passport

☐ 8 passport-sized photos – these always come in handy

☐ Visa paperwork for international students

☐ Birth certificate

☐ Exam certificates

☐ Topped-up phone card or Skype password

☐ All your bank stuff like chequebooks, paying-in books, past statements

☐ Oyster card if your university is in London – you can a get a student Oyster that gives you discounted fares

☐ National Insurance card

☐ Payslips and/or P45 and P60 – these will come in handy if you want to work alongside your studies

☐ NHS card or certificate – to sign up to doctor and dentist

☐ All your student finance paperwork

☐ Insurance documents for car, possessions etc.

☐ Any kind of tenancy agreement

☐ Television licence

> 💬 **Inside tip**
>
> **'Leave a copy of your new address at home. If anything needs to be redirected or sent to you it's quick and easy.'**
>
> *Dan, 21, Lancaster*

University stuff – you can buy a lot of this on campus

- [ ] Lined paper
- [ ] Sticky dots, drawing pins or Blu-Tack® – remember that Blu-Tack can leave stains on the wall and drawing pins make holes, so check with your university or landlord before you cover the walls with photos of nights out!
- [ ] Pencil case
- [ ] Pencils, sharpener, ruler and rubber
- [ ] Highlighters
- [ ] Permanent marker, for writing your name on all your stuff
- [ ] Scissors, hole punch, stapler
- [ ] Calculator – for all that budgeting
- [ ] A4 ring binders
- [ ] Notebooks
- [ ] Books from your reading list
- [ ] Personal books and magazines
- [ ] e-reader or tablet device if you have one, plus charger
- [ ] Dictionary and thesaurus
- [ ] Academic wall planner
- [ ] Postcards, writing paper and envelopes – postcards are a cheap, fun way to keep in touch
- [ ] Laptop, charger and case/sleeve
- [ ] External hard drive and USBs for keeping work backed up and secure
- [ ] Ethernet cable

Bathroom and bedroom stuff – check what your hall or accommodation already supplies

- [ ] Towels (hand and bath)
- [ ] Sponge, loofah, flannel etc.
- [ ] Shower gel
- [ ] Flipflops – for shared bathrooms
- [ ] Shaving equipment
- [ ] Toothbrush and toothpaste
- [ ] Shampoo and conditioner

University Life

- [ ] Deodorant
- [ ] Toilet roll – there may not be any in your room on the first day
- [ ] First aid kit – you never know when you may need it
- [ ] Painkillers – a fresher's must-have, whether it's the killer speakers or the hangover(s)
- [ ] Plant – optional
- [ ] Small bin for bathroom
- [ ] Cleaning products
- [ ] Wash basket
- [ ] Extension lead
- [ ] Plug adaptor if necessary
- [ ] Batteries
- [ ] Lamp
- [ ] Pinboard/whiteboard and pens
- [ ] Phone charger
- [ ] Alarm clock for when your phone dies
- [ ] Camera
- [ ] Music player docking station or speakers
- [ ] Headphones – I couldn't live without these in the library!
- [ ] Duvet
- [ ] Duvet covers and sheets
- [ ] Pillowcases
- [ ] Photos of family and friends
- [ ] Bean bag
- [ ] Sleeping bag – very handy for parties
- [ ] Laundry detergent/powder, fabric softener
- [ ] Hangers
- [ ] Kitchen and housekeeping stuff – again, check what is already there
- [ ] Bottle opener
- [ ] Cutlery
- [ ] Tin opener
- [ ] Weighing scales
- [ ] Measuring jug
- [ ] Toastie maker – for quick snacks

- [ ] Potato masher
- [ ] Pizza cutter (though large kitchen scissors work just as well)
- [ ] Grater
- [ ] Plates
- [ ] Cereal bowls
- [ ] Pans
- [ ] Kitchen foil
- [ ] Clingfilm
- [ ] Sieve
- [ ] Wok
- [ ] Steamer (really good for multitasking – can cook three layers of food, like vegetables, potatoes, even pasta)
- [ ] Colander
- [ ] Lasagne dish with lid – not just for lasagne, good for storing stuff too
- [ ] Oven tray
- [ ] Tea towel
- [ ] Blender
- [ ] Apron
- [ ] Loads of Tupperware or save and bring plastic takeaway boxes
- [ ] Mixing bowl
- [ ] Cake tray – cupcakes are always a winner at fundraising events
- [ ] Snacks for the first day

> (···) **Inside tip**
>
> 'I got loads of cooking stuff, like plates and spatulas, from the local charity shop. Everything was so cheap and I even picked up some funky vintage plates!'
>
> *Ashika, 20, York*

Recommended extras

- [ ] Torch – for finding your way back to your room at night
- [ ] Umbrella
- [ ] Board games – great for socialising and getting everyone together
- [ ] Superglue
- [ ] Earplugs
- [ ] Clothes horse for drying clothes
- [ ] Old school tie and afro wig for fancy dress

Now you have bought everything, remember to pack it carefully: heavy stuff like shoes go on the bottom of case, with the lighter items towards the top. Pack toiletries in plastic bags in case of any leakages.

'Holly was sure she had packed everything...'

Getting your student finances sorted out

I'm going to break this topic down into five easy sections.

Student loan

Getting a student loan is pretty much part of every student's life. You can get a tuition fee loan easy enough. You can also get a maintenance loan, which is there to contribute to your living costs, rent, food and anything else you need through your time at university.

According to www.direct.gov.uk, the amount you can borrow for a maintenance loan is relative to:

* your household income
* where you live
* when your start your course
* what year of study you're in
* what help you get, if any, through a maintenance grant (see below)

Tuition fee loans are available to both full- and part-time students, while maintenance loans are only available to full-time students. The best thing to do is to check out the relevant pages on www.direct.gov.uk: click on Education and learning. All the information about loans, including the current amount for the year you apply, can be found there. www.direct.gov.uk is also the website where you'll be starting your student finance application form.

Student finance forms can seem daunting at first. Here are some tips to help:

> Get all the forms you need from the www.direct.gov.uk website. If you make a mistake you can reprint the individual page, not the whole form.

> ⓘ **Need to know…**
> To get more info on going away to university and fees, visit www.studentfinance-yourfuture.direct.gov.uk.

> Make sure that you put the right address on the envelope, or if you are completing the form online make sure that you send it back way before the deadline.

> Check that all your personal information is correct, otherwise your application could be delayed.

> Write down or store the number for the student finance helpline – you'll need it.

> If you are going to call up student finance, try to use a phone with a loudspeaker – sometimes you may have to wait in a queue for 10 minutes or more and if you put the phone on speaker you can do something else.

> Print out a copy of your payment schedule and write it all down on your year planner. That way you know when to set up your direct debits for bills and other things you need to pay.

💬 **Inside tip**

'I found all the student finance stuff really confusing as there was just so much to look through, but one of my friends told me about our university finance officer. I tracked the officer down and gave them a ring – best thing I could have done. They were really helpful and answered all my questions. If you're stuck, definitely give your finance officer a try.' *Caroline, 22, Leeds*

Student grant

A student grant is money that you don't have to pay back. The amount you can get depends on your household income and it's your local education authority (LEA) that decides how much you receive. When you are applying make sure you include all your details correctly so that you can get the money that you're entitled to. If you are eligible to get a grant, do make sure that you apply for all of it. The extra will definitely come in handy for bills and rent or if there's an emergency.

Coming from a single-parent family there wasn't any spare cash to help me with university, and even though I worked in the summer holidays the grant really came in handy. I applied for the maximum amount I was entitled to so if I needed it, it was there.

For more information on both loans and grants, visit the Student Loans Company (SLC) at www.slc.co.uk.

Bursaries and scholarships

Most universities offer some sort of bursary, which is normally paid over the course of each academic year and you don't have to pay it back. Amounts do vary depending on your parents' income or your own, so your best bet is to give your university a ring or check its website for how much you may be entitled to. Most universities also offer extra money for students who come across hardship, so definitely do some digging around if you think you may be entitled to additional help.

If there is an opportunity to apply for a scholarship, go for it! You will usually have to have good A-level results to be a candidate for this, as many university scholarships are based on academic ability. The best way to go about seeing if you can get a scholarship is to look on your university website, as there will be links to the scholarships and awards that it currently offers.

Sponsorship

Surprisingly, there are many companies that will sponsor your studies. Some will even sponsor your whole degree if it is to do with the work you do for them. For example, a county council could potentially sponsor a youth worker to complete the degree if that youth worker is working exclusively for the council. It's amazing how much funding there actually is in the businesses around you. The best thing to do (after checking a company's website for any additional information) is to ask and see if it can help in any way. Each university has a different procedure for how the payments will be made and to whom, so have this information ready in case your potential sponsor wants to know more.

Some companies will pay for your studies if you're guaranteed to be working for them when you graduate. I know what it's like when you finish your degree, I was a very different person to when I first started out, and my career plans had changed quite a bit. So if you do allow a company to sponsor you and it makes this stipulation, make sure that you have taken this into consideration.

The army offers sponsorship with future employment as a condition. One of my friends joined the army and did a course in Information Technology that the armed forces ended up sponsoring substantially. If you want more information on this, check out www.armyjobs.mod.uk.

> ### Career builder
> Take in as much as possible about the process of getting ready to go to university. Can you use your experience to write a blog or become a student ambassador at your uni next year?

Disabled student support

If you have a disability, it's important to note that there is financial help that you may be entitled to. As a student you may have access to Disabled Student's Allowance from Student Finance England and Disability Living Allowance, which comes from the Disability and Carers Service.

To work out what you are entitled to and other support available, check out: www.direct.gov.uk/en/DisabledPeople/EducationAndTraining/HigherEducation/index.htm

Student bank accounts

With so many banks competing with each other for your student finances, it can be hard to see which one is best for you. My advice is: compare, compare, compare. Try to ignore the free mug or vouchers a bank is offering you to sign up and have a good think about what you really need your account for.

How big do you want your overdraft to be? Most banks offer a generous overdraft to students, but if you go over the agreed limit you may be landed with some hefty charges. Get all the information for each student account and compare them to see which one ticks the most boxes for you. Remember that just because your friend is going with a certain bank it doesn't mean you have to, and the bank you grew up with doesn't have to be the bank you stay with if there is a better offer elsewhere.

I used two great websites – www.moneysavingexpert.com and www.thestudentroom.co.uk – to see what other students thought was the best account and what each bank was offering. After that, I looked on all of the main high street bank websites to read up on the terms, conditions and, most importantly, the small print. Armed with all the information I could find, I then made my final decision.

> 💬 **Inside tip**
>
> 'Get a low overdraft to begin with, there's less temptation to overspend in the first few weeks and you can always raise it later in the year.' *Serhan, 19, London*

Keeping in touch

It is hard leaving family friends and even pets behind when you go to university. Everyone reacts differently to moving away. We're all different people with different lives and personalities. However, don't get down about saying goodbye, because thanks to technology, seeing your loved ones can be a matter of pressing a few buttons.

Staying in contact by visiting, phoning and texting are all ways to remain in the loop and share your experiences with your friends and family. Using other media like social networking sites and Skype is also great for catching up on news and seeing visual updates. Some smartphones have software that allows you to make face-to-face calls. It's important to keep your friendships and family links intact – when you come home in the holidays or need a chat that only you and that one person can have, you need still to have that important bond with the people closest to you.

If it suits you, starting up a blog is an easy way to keep the people you care about updated. Sites like Tumblr and Blogspot are good if you're more of a photo person, or not too keen on writing much. If you're an overseas student, I definitely recommend getting a Skype app or the program downloaded onto your computer. A lot of my friends who are international students swear by it – especially because it's free. I know that video calling can't replace being with someone, but it's a lifeline you'll need during the time you're away.

> **⊙ Inside tip**
>
> 'I was really homesick when my parents left on the first day so I called my best friend – she was going through the same thing and it really helped to have someone to talk about it with.'
>
> *Georgie, 21, Cardiff*

Getting ahead

Over the summer before you start university, tutors will send out lists of books you need to buy and read. To save you any hassle, I've compiled a few dos and don'ts to help you get ahead and feel more confident about your first wave of studying:

- ➷ Do buy the core texts and have a good read before you get to class.
- ➷ Do save money on your books – check out sites like Amazon, eBay or AbeBooks for secondhand copies.
- ➷ Do highlight sections in the books that you find useful. If you don't like marking your books, use different-coloured page markers to draw attention to the parts of the book you could use in assignments.

- ☙ Don't worry if you feel overwhelmed by the amount of reading you have to do. For example, if you need to read a whole novel by the time you get to university, break it down. Look for summaries on the internet so that if you don't finish the whole story, you have an idea of what the book's about.
- ☙ Do check your university's online library catalogue to see if it holds copies of the books you need. If they are in the library and you won't be using them very often, you may not need to buy them straight away.
- ☙ Don't worry. Your tutors will be able to give you more information on the work you'll be doing when you get to class.
- ☙ Do try to organise the information you have into folders for each module, or notebooks if you prefer.

Don't forget

Let your current bank and mobile phone provider know that you are moving from your current address, and update your addresses with other companies as necessary. Whether you live in halls or private housing, the last thing you want is your new clubbing outfit getting posted to your parents' house miles away! eBay, Amazon and other popular mail delivery sites will need your new address as soon as possible.

> I hope this chapter has really helped you feel more excited and less nervous about getting ready to go to uni. I know what it's like going away and meeting loads of new people – and agonising about what they might think of you, and whether you'll fit in or not. Try to replace your worries with positive thoughts like 'I'm going to make lots of friends and enjoy my time away. I'll be back in the holidays and want to have loads to tell everyone.' Remember, it's an adventure. You've got everything ready for the journey, so let's get to the next step – Freshers' Week!

2

Freshers

So, you've got your finances sorted, you're in your new pad, everything's unpacked (on the floor) and you're ready to get started at uni! This chapter covers all you need to know about Freshers' Week and, more importantly, how to get a head start in your new life.

You are now officially a fresher!

Your first Freshers' Week will be really busy: unpacking, dancing, eating, drinking and comparing timetables.

I walked into the freshers' fair alone and very nervous, but recognised someone who had been at the open day so I went and said hi. I had also joined a few university Facebook groups. Remember, as well as being a great place to make friends, the freshers' fair is a potential goldmine: I picked up a free pizza voucher, posters, a USB or two and a free colander. My advice is to be really open and try to check out a bit of everything. There will be loads of stalls and activities to choose from. Even if you haven't done something or even seen it before, take a look, it could be fun.

'Geoff knew that his afro wig would come in handy for something...'

Societies, sports and clubs

Lots of societies will be advertised at the freshers' fair – I remember seeing the Football Society, Student Newspaper and Debate Society. Definitely check them all out. There is usually a list available and they will probably have pages on Facebook, so you can try before you join. You don't *have* to join any societies, but it's a good idea to see who and what are out there. Don't forget to check out the sports clubs too. Rounders, hockey and athletics are just some of the sports clubs at most universities. As well as this being a good way to stay fit, you can meet new friends and enjoy some healthy competition.

The first few weeks can be overwhelming, but don't worry, it does calm down! See the first year as your time to get settled in, get to know others and get into your degree. Your first year should provide you with a strong foundation. If you are living in halls or a shared house, your roommates will probably become some of your closest friends. Even if they don't, there are plenty of other people to make friends with and get to know – such as people on your course and at clubs. Start by being approachable so that other students know it's okay to say hi.

If you are feeling homesick – and this is perfectly normal – then why not give your family or friends a ring, leave a comment on Facebook, or put some photos of your friends and family up in your room, if you haven't already.

> ### 💬 Inside tip
> **'Freshers is more than just a week of fun, there are so many events and parties to go to, you make loads of new friends and it's a great way to get into the uni lifestyle.'** *Gaz, 20, Bath*

> ### 💬 Inside tip
> **'Be aware of "Freshers' flu". Quite a few of my friends were struck down with a mysterious bad cold during the first few weeks of freshers. Stock up on flu remedies and see the doctor if it gets worse.'** *Michael, 25, Oxford*

> ### 💬 Inside tip
> **'Decide how much money you want to spend on Freshers' Week and stick to it. It's not cool when most of your rent money has gone on booze.'** *Chloe, 20, London*

Students' Union

The Students' Union is another great place to start making friends and networking. The Union is an organisation made up of students and can also be called a guild or association. It has a president, vice-president and many officers. For example, there is an officer to represent mature students, lesbian/gay/bi/transgender students, international students and so on. The positions within the Students' Union will vary, but you can be part of the organisation and even become an officer. It's a great place to get to know the other students and make a change in the university. If there's something you're passionate about, why not campaign to gain that position?

The Students' Union will also often have a bar or café, shop and even sports facilities. It's good to go down and have a look in Freshers' Week, even if just to mingle with others and see what you have in common.

> 💬 **Inside tip**
>
> 'I didn't really know what to expect from the Students' Union but went along anyway. The members were actually really helpful and had loads of tips and information on student rights and organisations I wouldn't have ever known about.'   *Faz, 19, Birmingham*

Lectures, seminars and tutorials

Lectures, seminars and tutorials are where you will pick up much of the learning that you will rely on in your second year. I must admit I did miss a few lectures, but I'll also admit that it was hard to catch up if I did. It's a bit like missing an episode of your favourite show – you have to backtrack and get filled in before you can move on.

Seminars and tutorials are shorter than lectures and are often more intimate, because of the smaller groups. Having to present your work can suck at first when you're new, but in the long run it's really beneficial. You also get a chance to know people better because you can all talk together, unlike lectures where you are mostly taking notes and listening.

Waking up late is a problem for many students, but even if you do, don't give up straight away. Is there an opportunity to join the lecture during a break? Never think it's too late to catch up.

When you are in a seminar, try to join in. Sometimes you may sit and listen, and that is fine; there may be so much going on in the week that you just want to be still. But you will gain so much information that you can use to add to the quality of your degree, so try to soak up as much as you can while you're there – and don't forget to take the handout!

Seminars can give you a great opportunity to get used to voicing your opinions in front of your peers, and you get a platform on which to display your work and open it up for criticism. You also get a chance to practise giving feedback on other people's work. Constructive criticism in a seminar environment is particularly important for creative writers who are starting out. You'll have your very own friendly group that will comment on your work and hopefully help you make it even better.

(⁝⁝) **Inside tip**

'I went to lectures but skipped quite a few seminars because I thought they were less important – big mistake. I missed out on sharing my work with everyone else and didn't get the feedback I needed to help me make it better. If could change anything about my first year it would be not skipping classes.'

Yinka, 21, Bristol

Taking notes

Not everyone takes notes, but doing so does help you. If you had a late night it's going to be difficult to remember what was said in the lecture. If you're late but your friends have been taking notes, you could ask to photocopy theirs. Then you can slot them into your folder and refer to them when writing up your assignments.

Lecturers can share a lot of wisdom in lectures. They know what will help you achieve the best grade you can, and remember, they've been through it already, so make the most of what they're telling you.

> ### 💬 Inside tip
> 'Type up all of the quotations you could possibly use for an essay. These quotations will usually be things you underlined or highlighted when reading the text which are relevant to your essay question. This process is time consuming, but it ultimately makes it much quicker and easier to see what is and isn't going to be useful. You can then arrange the quotations you want thematically so that an essay structure with themed paragraphs will emerge. Everyone plans essays differently but this works very well for me.'
>
> *Alice, 21, Kingston*

Laptops and notebooks

I would suggest getting a small, light laptop if possible. If you're unsure which model to buy, it's helpful to speak to an adviser in your nearest high street computer shop. They know what they're talking about and can save you hours of searching. If you want an even more in-depth review of the laptop you are interested in, check out YouTube. There are thousands of laptop reviews up there and often you can see the laptop or notebook actually opened and used.

And remember to investigate whether educational discounts are available for the computer and software you need, either before you start or once you're on campus.

The faculty

Your degree subject will fit within a faculty. For example, an English degree will slot into the faculty of arts or humanities. If you are doing a joint degree, you might be under two faculties, such as arts and social sciences. Keep your eye out for the student reps in your faculty at the freshers' fair.

There may also be a society for your particular degree, and if there is it can't hurt to join. You can learn from your peers and interact with them. You never know what opportunities can arise from networking with new people. If there isn't such a society, maybe later in the year you could, with a few other like-minded students, form your own? To do this, contact whoever heads up the university's societies. Drum up support by printing posters and by word of mouth. Make use of social networks to set up groups online where people can interact and keep up to date with the kind of events you may want to put on.

Faculties also run special talks, lectures or social events. Make sure that you sign up to your faculty's email list or check your university email inbox for notifications. Often the talks and lectures will feature a guest or specialist speaker who may be able to shed some light on something you have been studying. I remember a guest speaker who inspired me to create an anthology! Keep up to date with your faculty's social calendar.

> ### 💬 Inside Tip
> **'Don't feel nervous about speaking with the staff in your faculty. They know what they're talking about and are really helpful, especially with paperwork!'**
>
> *Elle, 26, London*

> ### 💬 Inside tip
> **'In my first year I belonged to the film society. Being involved really helped me come up with ideas for my screenwriting module and make new friends.'**
>
> *Jay, 32, Manchester*

Your faculty will have a specific office and a course administrator. If you need information or help it is likely to be much quicker to go to them because they already know your name, course, year, details and so on. The faculty office also often holds all the module lists. You'll be doing different modules for each year of your degree, and there are deadlines for when you can choose them. If you can get hold of copies of all the module lists for your course early on, you are more likely to be able to take the module you want. Some modules were really popular on my course and we were advised to choose a few months earlier than the deadline.

If you get the modules early you can also see what options there are for your final year, which will include your dissertation. You may think it's too soon to be thinking about this, but your dissertation probably has the highest word count of any assignment in your degree, so it makes sense to get a head start. Dissertation options vary from university to university, so make sure that you plan your module selection to accommodate what you are likely to want to write about.

If you are crafty, you could start planning your dissertation in your first year and continue it up into your third year. If there's a topic you really enjoyed in your first or second year, it could be inspiration for a later project.

Office hours and making appointments

Office hours are the times when your lecturers are available to meet and talk with you. In your module guide, along with the week-by-week schedule of the course, your lecturer's office hours should be explained. Get to know your lecturers in your first year and if you have an issue to discuss or a problem you wish to raise, do visit them in office hours. It is best to email your lecturer just to make sure they are free to meet you. They may also need to rearrange the time or place at short notice, so keep checking your emails.

> 💬 **Inside tip**
>
> **'Don't worry if a lecturer doesn't get back to you straight away, they probably have hundreds of emails to check each week – be patient or go and visit them if you need an answer straight away.**
>
> *Sarah, 21, Bath*

Each teacher will communicate differently. If you don't appreciate a lecturer's style, don't just shut off. They have prepared a lecture for you, will most probably be marking your work, and will ultimately be adding to your final degree classification. It's often easy as a student to forget that your lecturers have already done their degree, not to mention their Master's and PhD. They know what they are talking about, so listen to them.

Study skills centres

Another place to visit is your study skills centre, where you can go and get help with your assignments. The advisers are trained to look for certain errors and will help you learn how to rectify them. Get used to taking your plans and assignments there for a once over, make changes and bring them back again. Get to know the advisers or choose an adviser to take your work to on a regular basis. Then they will be familiar with your style and probably advise you a lot more quickly.

It's been said that a visit to your skills centre can improve your work by one whole grade and from my experience working in an academic centre I would definitely agree. Another pair of eyes is always better for spotting spelling mistakes and grammatical errors. Advice can also be given on other study skills such as reading and revising for exams.

📖 The inside story: Maryam

'When starting university, I knew it would be challenging and difficult and did not feel I would receive as much attention concerning my work as I had in A-level. When I got to uni I was introduced to a scheme called CASE (Centre for Academic Support and Employability). This centre is where professional academic advisers have a look at pieces of coursework and help you to achieve the best grade you can. I have been attending ever since, and find the centre really useful. I continue to encourage colleagues to attend this as the advisers do make a real difference. The knowledge and confidence I took away from CASE have enabled me to write clearly and structure my work in a coherent form. Alongside seeking help from the advisers I read study skills books, as I know this will affect the grade I receive from university and therefore help me in my future career.'

Maryam makes university work for her by using all the resources on offer – make sure you do too!

Help!

As well as staff who can help with your work, there are also trained staff who can help with your life. University life can get stressful, which is why there will be a chaplain, helpline or mentor who can offer help and support. If things are getting too tough and you don't want to talk to friends about it, how about booking an appointment with the chaplain? Chaplains are trained ministers who offer spiritual care to anyone who needs it in the university.

Most universities also offer personal help through a helpline or nightline. There will be trained operators on standby to offer advice with your problems. Alternatively, if you prefer face-to-face help your university may offer a mentoring programme that you may want to use.

In addition, tutors and lecturers can often help with ways to relieve pressure, as they have been through a degree themselves. If there is a lecturer or tutor you trust, perhaps drop them an email and book an appointment with them in their office hours. A lot of my stress was related to the amount of work I had to do for my assignments and keeping to deadlines. I found that when I had discussed these issues with a lecturer, they didn't seem so scary and I didn't feel so alone. Talking with friends you can trust is also a good idea, as often you're all going through the same thing.

The library

With computers, online library catalogues, journals and magazines, it's a lot easier to get what you need from your university library (often called an LRC or learning resource centre). Not to mention there's a massive collection of DVDs to watch with your mates.

The library catalogue list all the books, DVDs, CDs, ebooks, journals, dissertations, videos and cassettes that are in the library. If your university has other campuses, their library catalogues will often be combined with yours. Make sure that you note where the book you are looking for is held.

Many students don't know that the LRC holds dissertations. Although you may have to ask an assistant to access them for you, don't let that stop you. Dissertations are very useful for getting ahead as a fresher. You will be working towards writing up your own dissertation or special study in your last year, so definitely check out what's been done before you for guidance.

I worked in my university library and got to know a few things that still helped me even in my third year. Here are my top five tips:

- ➷ If you need a book and it's out on loan, reserve it – you'll be notified when it's returned and it will be kept for you.
- ➷ Some books may be highlighted in the catalogue as available, but you may not be able to find them on the shelf. Check the overflow trolleys and the books that people have left on desks – you may find them there.
- ➷ If your item is at another campus, don't let that dissuade you from borrowing it. Universities will normally do inter-campus loans.
- ➷ Most DVDs have a lock system and are locked while on the shelves. When you take a DVD out, don't forget to unlock it before you go. I've done it before – popcorn, low lighting and then *The Godfather* just doesn't want to open up.
- ➷ Always check your library account regularly for books you have ordered, how many books you have on loan, when they're due back and any fines.

> 💬 **Inside tip**
>
> 'If you want to use a computer for a certain amount of time in the library, definitely book one in advance. If you can't get a booking, visit one of the IT rooms and log on there to do your work – it's quieter and a lot less busy.'
>
> *Pete, 19, Exeter*

Electronic learning

The library isn't the only place you can access your university intranet and the university wifi. You'll get assigned a username and password. If you have a laptop you can log in to the intranet wherever you are, on campus or at home.

Keep a look out for new apps if you have a smartphone. I downloaded a free books app that allowed me to read over 1000 classic titles on my phone.

Podcasts and ebooks are really handy for catching up when you're on the go. I track new downloads down by typing what I'm looking for into a search engine, then saving the webpage as a bookmark. Check your selected sites regularly to make the most of elearning while you're out and about.

> (···) **Inside tip**
>
> 'As a commuter, I invested in a netbook for uni. It was small enough to fit into my handbag and easy to carry around as well as being cheaper than a full-size laptop. It allowed me to do everything I needed for uni, e.g. searching the web, typing up lecture notes, and it's a lot faster to type than write for most.'
>
> *Sofiya, 21, Kingston*

Style guides

Each university has its own style guides to which different faculties adhere. For example, when I do any assignment it must adhere to the MHRA (Modern Humanities Research Association) style guide. The margins, headers and footers must be in a certain place. My work must be spaced at a certain amount, my bibliography must be ordered correctly and my footnotes must be set out in the designated way. There will be a link to the relevant style guides on your university website and there should be copies in your library.

It's definitely worth printing out your style guide and using it alongside your assignments – especially in the first year where everything is so different from A-Level work.

> (···) **Inside tip**
>
> 'If all the partying and studying gets too much, have a movie night. Make popcorn and get your box sets lined up, then invite a few friends over to your place.'
>
> *Gemma, 19, Durham*

Does the first year really count?

It does! Fair enough, your marks are not carried over towards your degree, but you should still see your first year as your first chance. You can spend your time well or you can waste it. Use your first year to build a network of good friends and good places to go. Having a network is useful because as a student you need trusted people who will give you honest feedback about your work, lecturers who can make suggestions tailored to your needs, and like-minded friends who will help pull you up rather than let you down.

☺ **Pocket money generator**

Can you use your experience as a fresher to become a freshers' welcomer at your uni next year? Relive Freshers' Week and earn a few bob – sounds good to me!

In my first year I really made an effort to get to know my classmates and lecturers. This led to me helping to start up our college's first ever open mic session, which is still flourishing to this day. But I couldn't have done that without getting to know my lecturers and classmates. A network isn't built overnight, but in your first year you can lay a good foundation. That will give you a good starting point for your second year, which is when your marks will begin to count towards your final degree classification.

Freshers' Week is just the start of your degree and there will be fun, challenges and new experiences. You'll find that many crazy times happen in halls of residence. Commonly called 'party central', halls are where you'll be sleeping, living and chilling.

The next chapter will guide you through the ups and downs of living in halls and houses and help you settle into your new home.

3

Halls and Housing

Halls are most likely where you'll spend your first year of uni; you may then be in your own pad with your mates in your second and third years. The challenges and experiences you'll face are all part of being independent and living away from home as a student. This chapter is packed full of all the help you'll need.

Accommodation

Living in a hall of residence is a good place to start your university life because there are other students close by. It's also often safer to be in halls rather than in a house in a new area you don't know. If you have a disability, halls will be mobility friendly. More often than not you will have the campus office and perhaps even a caretaker and cleaner to help keep things working smoothly. Best of all, you can stay in the loop as to when there are gatherings and events happening on and off campus.

The fees you pay for accommodation at university often cover utility bills as well. The due dates are often timed to coincide with your student loan instalments, so you should be able to budget without complication.

It is rarer to live in a house in your first year, but it does happen. If you do move into a house instead of halls, make sure that it's close to halls or your campus so you can stay in touch with university life easily.

If you have any last-minute concerns, speak to the accommodation officer at your university. They'll be able to help you with all the official stuff and may have some handy tips to help you along. Check out the Useful Resources section at the back of this book for a list of websites to help you find accommodation throughout university.

Of course, you can always live at home if your campus is within reasonable travelling distance. It's a lot cheaper than living elsewhere, but you do miss out on the whole 'starting out as an independent student' experience, which can be a helpful initiation into university life and prepare you for the next few years of study.

If you do decide to live at home while at university, even if it's just for your first year, here are a few tips:

- Help out around the house. Even if you're living with a relative, you must remember to treat them with respect.

> **⌨ Inside tip**
> **'I found living in halls noisy, messy and just a wee bit crazy – but it was worth it!'**
> *Terry, 21, Edinburgh*

- Socialise with your student mates and go to your society and club meetings to keep up with everyone else.
- Save, save, save! If you're not paying rent, you're in a position that many students aren't. You should be able to save a lot of money, so put it aside in an online savings account or ISA to keep it safe.
- Invest in a good sleeping bag or blow-up mattress (get the one with the electric pump attachment) to take with you so you can stay with friends overnight. Your parents might get a

little annoyed with you coming home at 4am most nights of your first year!

ל If you're living at home to save money, stick it out. It may be hard sometimes, but keep in mind the money you're saving towards a year of travelling or the house deposit you'll have available when you graduate.

ל Enjoy and appreciate your time with your family. Most students have to leave their family and will miss them a lot.

> **☉ Inside tip**
>
> **'Be prepared to meet all different types of people at uni. Try not to stick with what you're used to otherwise you'll miss out on new experiences.'**
>
> *Paige, 19, London*

📖 The inside story: Becca

'I remember the day that I needed to leave for university. I found it strange and surreal that all my belongings seemed to fit inside Mum's tiny Vauxhall Corsa. I always thought I had more to show for my 18 years of living and it had finally hit me that I wouldn't be living with my family for the next three years. Also it was bittersweet, because more than the lack of material possessions was the fact that I was happy and excited to leave my family behind and start my life.

The entire journey there, I had a niggling feeling that I wouldn't be able to make friends with the other six people I would be living with and that the first year we'd all just reside together and never speak...

Luckily, I remembered a helpful tip from my college form tutor, who said that the best way to strike up a conversation with someone you don't know is to ask them for something. For example, you ask to borrow a teabag or, if they're in the same class, to look at the timetable.

I've never been so grateful to my form tutor. That piece of advice has stayed with me and when the time came for me to introduce myself to my flatmate, Jeni, I did the simplest thing and asked to borrow a teabag and milk to make a cup of tea for my mum who, after helping me unpack and sort out my room, was in desperate need of some TLC. Asking for something like this breaks the tension and awkwardness of being the 'new person' and it shows the other flatmates who you are: confident and easy to talk to.

The best way to feel comfortable while living in halls is to make your room homely and yours. This is quite simply because you'll be living in there for the following year(s) until you finish your course or move out into student housing for your second and third years.

I had brought with me photographs of my family members in frames and had them featured on one of my main shelves so that I could see them every time I walked in and out of my room. I had the idea that I wouldn't miss them as much if I could always see them.

Each room was fitted with a pin board that stretched across one of the walls and I decided that it would be a great idea to fill it with the things that define me. I had small pictures of handsome actors, my photography work from college, old family photos and other items that I had collected or had been given to me because people had seen them and thought of me. All these memories and landmarks in my life were all collected together on this pin board. The best thing about having a personal mood board is that when you look at it, you instantly remember that specific time or person and you feel better about yourself.

Some people find it hard to live away from home. When my other flatmates' families left them a few cried the whole night, but then there will be those who have no feelings of regret. My advice is to let people deal with their feelings in their own way; you may cry or you may lock yourself in your room or you may be perfectly fine. Just remember that you're all feeling similar emotions being away from home, and that you shouldn't be embarrassed because other people should understand exactly what you're going through.'

📖 **The inside story: Karee**

'I'm from Chicago and I noticed during my time abroad in London how imperative it was to engage with my classmates and truly get to know the culture. When you take the time to get to know people, you have an extremely rewarding experience, and friends that could last a lifetime.

I lived with a land-lady; it was an experience I would recommend, because it gives you more of a comforting environment to live in when you're away from home. It also helps you learn and appreciate British culture.'

Laundry

The whole process of doing the laundry is something you have to learn if you've never done it before. My first wash was diabolical – I put all my coloured clothes on a hot wash and the colour faded out of them. Most clothing will have washing instructions on the label (which I didn't even think to check!), but just in case here are some handy hints to get you started:

💬 **Inside tip**

'If you do have to use the launderette, keep change aside in a jar so that you're never caught short. Also keep small plastic pots for putting the powder in so you don't have to lug the whole box with you.'

Bethan, 19, Cardiff

ⓘ **Need to know...**

Check out www.ariel.co.uk/LaundryTips/Default.aspx for tips on how to wash your clothes, use fabric softeners and washing temperatures.

- ꙮ Don't let it all pile up – practice makes perfect.
- ꙮ Empty your pockets first. Phones don't normally work after going through the wash!
- ꙮ Take a look at the labels – sometimes they will give information about washing special materials like wool or silk.
- ꙮ Don't mix whites with colours of any kind – especially not red.
- ꙮ On the washing machine there will usually be symbols to

show you where powder and fabric softener go – if in doubt, ask someone. Don't feel silly, because everyone has to learn.

❧ If you need something immediately, wear rubber gloves and hand wash it in a basin, bucket or the sink with washing powder. Try not to waste water, energy and electricity on just a few items.

If you're doing your washing in the campus launderette, use some kind of timer so you can collect it as soon as it's done.

Finding a new place

Towards the end of your first year it's likely that you'll be starting to look for a new house share or flat to live in through your second and third years of university. This can be tricky, so I've included in this section all the things I learnt along the way.

Student accommodation can sometimes be rundown, so make sure that the roof and window frames are sound. There shouldn't be any slipped tiles (this could result in a leak) or rotten window frames (this will definitely result in a leak – and probably all over your new outfit that's drying on the radiator). I know that sometimes you aren't going to be able to do more than have a quick look in each room, but be aware of what fresh paint can cover. Have a good sniff around – literally. Do any of the rooms (especially on the ground floor) smell damp – like

> 💬 **Inside tip**
>
> 'Ask the landlord what you can and can't do, like painting or removing furniture, before you move in.' *Rachel, 21, Cambridge*

musty old wet leaves? Black mould and peeling wallpaper are also dead giveaways. Even a small patch of mould can grow and spread. The spores in mould are also very harmful and can lead to respiratory problems if it is left to fester and grow. Don't put a cheap price over your health.

Check that the property includes white goods, like a fridge, freezer, washing machine and dishwasher. If there isn't a washing machine, how close is the launderette and how much does it cost? If it's a long way, cost and hassle are going to be involved in getting your clothes clean and dry.

Something a lot of my friends forgot to ask about was the gas certificate. Every landlord should have an up-to-date gas safety certificate following an inspection carried out by an engineer who is on the Gas Safe Register.

Who pays?

You need to know what you are expected to pay for and what your landlord is going to contribute as part of the rent. This is very important, otherwise bills could arrive unexpectedly and wipe you out for that month. Questions to ask your prospective landlord include:

- Who pays to clear out gutters?
- Who pays to fix leaky windows?
- Who pays for damage to furniture?
- Who pays for the gardener?

When you move out of halls, be sure to grab a council tax exemption form. As a student, even if you're living at home, you don't need to pay council tax. Ask at your university for the form and for more information.

> ### 💬 Inside tip
> 'Don't put all the bills in your name; work out a system that is fair on all parties before you move in. If you do and a few of the others don't pay on time, the non-payments on your account can damage your credit score.'
>
> *Jordon, 22, Manchester*

Landlords

Landlords can be tricky. They're out to make money, not necessarily for your benefit. So before you sign anything regarding a rental property, make sure that you do your research. This is a big investment of your money, so ensure that you're paying the right person for the right things. Instead of trying to check yourself, first go to the accommodation officer at university to see what advice they give.

When you have decided on a property, get your landlord's personal contact number and address, as well as details of any caretaker, cleaner or handyman in case there's an emergency.

Make sure that you can transfer all the bills into your name straight away (or to whomever you have all agreed) so you can't be liable for previous tenants' bills or outstanding payments for maintenance.

Get a list of everything that comes with the house or flat. This is called an inventory. The last thing you want is to be slapped with a £50 bill for the plate you broke, not knowing it was an antique.

Insurance

Pretty much everyone is going to have a laptop in the house as well as a television, perhaps a guitar or two and other goodies that burglars will just love. Especially when you're out at lectures and parties, leaving ample time for break-ins. The first and essential tip is to get insured. The second is to get everything from your laptop backed up. I know it may seem annoying to have to save everything on a USB or have an identical hard drive as back-up, but it's going to save you time, trouble and a shedload of stress if you do it – and do it consistently. It's always that one time you can't be bothered that ends up costing you.

> ☺ **Pocket money generator**
>
> Could you be a top student landlord when you graduate? You know the ropes, know the area and have been through it all before, so you know what students want. Could you get some investments or trusted friends on board, buy a house and let the rent per room pay off the mortgage? Do some research, speak to successful people who have done it already and see what you can do.

Endsleigh provides specialist student insurance, which takes landlords and previous claims into account. Check out the website www.endsleigh.co.uk for more information. You can also get household insurance from your bank.

Safety and security

First things first, don't give your key out to anyone. They could easily make a copy and come and go as they please.

Remember that it's not just your stuff at stake, there are other people living with you. Make sure that you all agree on this and have a specific keyholder for the spare key to avoid any bother. Also ask your landlord if all the previous tenants gave their keys back – the last thing you want is someone camping out in your living room while you're away.

Make sure that you lock your door and windows when you leave your house, as this could lead to an easy break-in. If you do come home to a break-in, report it to the police immediately and let your landlord and housemates know. Also lock valuables away in a safe place when you have parties.

Housemates

> 💬 **Inside tip**
>
> 'We got a kitty together at the start of each semester for things like bin bags, washing-up liquid, toilet paper and bleach. That way there were always cleaning products in the house and if they run out there's no excuse for not buying more!'
>
> *Bola, 24, Sheffield*

You can't choose who is close to your personal space in student halls of residence, but you often can in private housing. One of my friends described her housemates as lazy, sloppy and downright rude; another said hers were now her best mates. I even know over-60s who are still friends with people they shared their student digs with.

> 📖 **The inside story: Daisy's top 5 housing dilemmas and how she solved them**
>
> 1 In my second year I lived in a house with really dodgy heating. My room was always freezing and the rest of the house refused to have the heating on higher and for longer, because it cost so much and their rooms were fine. My advice is to invest in an electric heater and have it next to your bed. Switch it on for ten minutes before getting out of bed on a winter morning.

2 One flatmate had a habit of throwing up in communal areas after nights out – in the corridor, on sofas, in the kitchen. Always ensure that you have a stash of bleach (because people like this never clean up properly after themselves) and incense or scented candles to help get rid of the smell!

3 When you live in halls, some people find it funny to set off the fire alarm in the middle of the night. My advice is not to worry about what you're wearing, but don't forget to grab an umbrella on your way out – being sleepy *and* getting soaked at 2 in the morning isn't fun.

4 Housemates who don't clean can be a nightmare, so check what their habits are before you all move in together if you can. I had to resort to eating in my room, as I refused to keep cleaning up after other people. One housemate couldn't even eat in the house!

5 A mean landlord tried to get out of paying me my deposit back. He promised for months to put it in the post and kept 'forgetting'. I called him continually for about three months and did eventually get my money back.

> ### ⌨ Inside tip
> **'Living in a house with my friends was a lot of fun. Just make sure you set out all the rules in the first few weeks so everyone's on the same page.'**
> *Ling, 20, Leeds*

Sharing the kitchen

Love them or hate them, you're going to be sharing your space with many other people. Sharing the kitchen is often the biggest cause for concern. I've collated some complaints below and offered advice to avoid dramas – and spillages.

☜ Keep cleaning products where they are easily accessible and can be seen – a brightly coloured bucket or wacky gloves may encourage regular cleaning.

- Keep your cleaning products gunk free – no one wants to use the 'salmonella cloth'.
- Use a 'hair trap' for the shower if you're sharing a bathroom. This handy device keeps the plughole clear.
- Kitchen roll is more hygienic to use on small spillages than a tea towel.
- Unless the university or landlord has provided you with a good bin, club together and buy a plastic roll-top bin. The pedal ones often break and have annoying parts that catch on the bin bag and split it.
- Keep the bin bags and recyling boxes close to the bin and recycle what you can.

There's a lot to think about when you're looking for somewhere to live; even when you get there, it seems that the questions keep on coming. Don't feel afraid to ask your parents or landlord loads of questions – it will save time in the long run.

Choose your housemates wisely and they may also be able to help you out too.

Another very important part of university life is food, which is where we go in the next chapter.

4

Food

I have to admit that I did end up nearly living on takeaways and pasta in my first year at uni. But the time did come when I just didn't have the money for takeaway food every week.

I started to learn how to cook, shop and budget for real food. It took a while, but I got there in the end. Don't worry if you feel clueless about food – it's all new and exciting to many people and it's completely normal to learn along the way.

In this chapter I share my tried-and-tested advice, student tips, and even a few fail-safe, easy-on-the-pocket recipes, so dig in.

A balanced diet

We've all heard of 'getting your five a day', but what exactly does this mean?

The term 'five a day' applies to the amount of fruit and vegetables you should include in your daily food intake. The suggested amount is five 80 gram portions a day – not five of veg and then another five of fruit, a mixture of veg and fruit. Eating fruit and vegetables is going to make you feel healthier and will have a positive effect on your appearance and possibly your weight.

I had a friend who swore that bananas were brain food; blueberries were also quite popular at one point for increasing brain activity. But does anything really make a difference? You'll have to learn what works best for you.

As well as fruit and vegetables, you should eat a variety of foods from the other four food groups: starchy food (rice, pasta, potatoes, bread); protein (meat, fish, eggs, beans); dairy food and eggs; foods containing fat and sugar.

The main thing about having a balanced diet at university is finding what works with your dietary needs and your time schedule – everyone is different. But when I was eating healthily, or at least watching how many fatty foods I was eating, I did feel a lot better about myself and a lot more alert in lessons.

Don't forget water. Keeping hydrated is really important in order to keep your concentration levels up. Replace energy drinks with smoothies and invest in a good water bottle. For a while, to save on costs, I used to reuse a branded plastic bottle, but after reading about the bacteria that tends to live in them I changed to a proper water bottle specifically designed to be reused – and I washed it in hot soapy water daily to keep the bugs at bay.

Remember the following tips about food:

ⓘ **Need to know...**

If you want to know more about getting your five a day as well as all things health, check out the official 5 A Day page on the National Health Service website: **www.nhs.uk/LiveWell/5ADAY**

💬 **Inside tip**

'My tip is to use a cookbook at university. Me and my housemates tried out the recipes together and it was such a laugh learning to cook.' *Adè, 21, London*

- If you eat takeaways all the time, it will cost you in the long term, physically and financially.
- Food can bring people together – use some of the recipes in this chapter like sharing fajitas to create a chilled social atmosphere.
- You don't have to be a gourmet chef or have any training to cook for yourself at university. You can learn from family, friends and definitely cookbooks and the internet.
- Food is meant to be fun. Something you may think is a mistake could turn out to be really tasty.

Budgeting

One of the most important things I learnt as a student was how to budget. I saved a lot of money on food shopping and here's how you can too.

When you get your student loan, grant and/or wages, take out the right amount for your rent and utility bills, and your food money, and put it aside. That way you won't end up living off beans for the last two weeks of the month.

If you buy from the right places, you can save a lot on your food bill. Budget how much you have to spend each month – this will fluctuate depending on how often you're going out, when the sales start or if higher bills and unexpected events happen. Check out Chapter 6, Managing, Making and Saving Money at university, for a sample monthly budget plan and more advice on how to save money.

Small things like bringing a thermos of tea or coffee to university instead of buying drinks throughout the day at the cafeteria can really make a difference to the money you have for food shopping. It's best to invest in a good strong thermos though, so it won't leak if your bag gets knocked in class.

> 💬 **Inside tip**
> 'Always have a large supply of pasta – it's really cheap and fills you up.'
> *Imran, 20, Bristol*

> 💬 **Inside tip**
> 'Me any my housemates were quite close so opted to do at least one or two of our big shops together on the internet. We shared the total and delivery charge. It was cheaper than carting all the food back ourselves or driving there and back. We were skint most of the time so this worked best for us. Oh, and using the 'mysupermarket' website saved us loads of time by displaying the cheapest supermarket to buy from that week.'
> *Dylan, 23, Glamorgan*

Where to shop

💬 **Inside tip**

'Sometimes packaged items are a lot cheaper loose, and sometimes loose items are more expensive than packaged. It's just a case of stepping out and trying new things.'

Kay, 21, Newcastle

When you have to shop for yourself you start to see how much money food actually costs. You can use supermarkets, pound shops and markets all at once – you don't have to stick to just one, so explore what's available in your area.

Here are seven golden rules for shopping well:

1 Get vegetables and bulk items at shops like Lidl or Aldi. Street markets are great too, but the times they open and close may not be ideal for students.

2 Bargain stores and pound shops are also good for food items and sundries like loo rolls and toothpaste. Take a look around in your first few weeks and find what works for you – maybe take along a friend to explore together.

3 Buying meat is a tricky area, since you often have to buy in larger quantities than you need. I looked longingly at the butcher's as a first-year student, but found that frozen meat or frozen tofu worked best for me and my friends. Check out the food hygiene section in this chapter to see how to defrost frozen meat safely.

4 Become a bargain hunter – at the end of each day a lot of food becomes discounted at supermarkets. I once found fresh broccoli for 11p! Scoop up the bargains and if something is freezable, make sure you stick to it, then defrost it when you want it and eat it the same day.

5 Supermarket versions of a branded item can be just as good – but they can also be worse. Try them out and see which you prefer. Some items just don't taste the same, but you may be able to stretch your palate and your pocket by buying supermarket own brands.

6 Buy a reusable bag for taking home your food shopping – it's better for the environment and makes carrying your items a lot easier.
7 If you constantly shop at a popular supermarket, why not sign up to its points system? Major supermarkets often have a points card on which you can get points from buying their items. These points can be converted into money-off vouchers or fun things like days out, or discounts off future purchases.

☺ **Pocket money generator**

Can you use your shopping skills to earn a few bob? If there are people less able than you to do their own shopping, perhaps you can do a weekly shop for them, earn some change and get to know someone new in return.

Writing a shopping list

Making a shopping list is the best way to go about it, trust me. I have tried to remember everything and I always forgot those two or three items I really needed. It doesn't have to be an especially amazing list, just go round your home and see what you need. If it's during your first week, have a look at your cupboard and fridge/freezer space first. This may determine how often you shop and how much you buy, so remember to take that into consideration. And don't forget to bring a pen to tick off what you put in your basket or trolley.

💬 **Inside tip**

'Invest in one of those shopping trolleys you see grannies with. They are ace for carting your food shopping back home and also double up for lugging books around uni.'

Carly, 22, London

Student staples

In our kitchen cupboards we always had the staples of rice, potatoes, cereal, bread, beans and other things we always needed. Here's a list of recommendations:

- Eggs
- Rice – easy cook is quickest, brown or granary is healthiest
- Potatoes – white potatoes are cheapest and make tasty chips, big ones can be baked with fillings; keep them out of the light otherwise they sprout
- Pasta
- Cereal – a quick, easy snack and only a bowl and spoon to wash up!
- Bread
- Ketchup
- Oil
- Butter/margarine
- Herbs (I went for mixed)
- Cans of beans
- Tuna
- Egg noodles and soy sauce – must-haves for a quick stir-fry
- Salt and pepper
- Vinegar
- Onions and garlic
- Stock cubes

> ⌐💬 **Inside tip**
>
> **'One thing I learnt at uni was how many meals you can do with one roast chicken! Soup, chicken salad sandwiches and stir-frys were just a few of the ones I discovered.'**
>
> *Chris, 28, Liverpool*

'Ian underestimated the lengths that Sam would go to...'

There was an odd mix in our fridge, always including unrecognisable jars at the bottom! Maybe pickles? Anyway, fresh, frozen and fridge items that we couldn't live without were the following:

- ⟡ Frozen vegetables like broccoli or peas – much cheaper than fresh and last longer
- ⟡ Fresh vegetables for specific recipes
- ⟡ Tinned tomatoes
- ⟡ Mince
- ⟡ Mushrooms
- ⟡ Cheese (can be frozen)
- ⟡ Frozen chicken pieces – can be cut up and used in stir-frys, sandwiches or tortillas
- ⟡ Sausages – cheap and flavoursome
- ⟡ Ice cubes – a necessity for parties, hot days and cooling down soup quickly

> **⟨⟩ Inside tip**
>
> 'When food starts to smell weird or turn a funny colour, it's time to throw it out! Always be sure to follow the use-by date and any storage instructions given on food labels to avoid the risk of food poisoning.'
>
> *Richard, 26, Manchester*

Kitchen equipment

These are the essentials, but see the ultimate packing list in Chapter 1 for more:

- Bottle opener – a must for student life!
- Handheld food blitzer – good for smoothies and soups

Blender	Saucepans (with lids)	Baking trays
Chopping board		Tin opener
Sharp knives	Frying pan	Wok

Organising your food

When packing your shopping at the checkout, put breakable things like eggs and loaves of bread on top of everything else in the bag so that they don't get crushed, and cans and tins on the bottom so that they can't crush anything. Fruit, vegetables and bread should be in one bag together so that they don't get damaged or squashed.

Each person puts things away differently and if you have to share your space it can get messy. I'm not saying that every label has to face the front and be just so (although I find this makes life a lot easier for me), but do try to stack things neatly. Clean the base of your cupboard to avoid pests and rodents. In the fridge, don't place raw meat above other food as the meat juices could drip, and keep cooked and raw foot separate.

💬 Inside tip

'When I first got to halls, those of us sharing the kitchen sat down and decided how we were going to share out space. Definitely one thing I would suggest is each having your own separate shelves in the fridge and freezer. That way people's food doesn't get mixed up. We also used different-coloured washing-up bowls for each person so the sink wasn't piled high with crusty dishes!'

Nazife, 20, Durham

💬 Inside tip

'Keep the clear plastic boxes you get at the takeaway – they're handy for storing leftovers and are free!'

Sheilagh, 29, Preston

Food hygiene

When you've just come in tired out from lectures, the last thing you want to do is to have to clear a clean space in the kitchen so that you can make your food. Here are a few tried-and-tested tips that made it easier for me and my housemates to avoid food poisoning and cook safely in the same kitchen. I may have watched too many episodes of *How Clean Is Your House?*, but as daft or simple as some of these sound, they really do work.

- At the start of term, decide on a cleaning rota so that the kitchen stays as clean and tidy as possible.
- Stick your tea towels and cleaning cloths in the washing machine whenever you do a wash – that way they won't get gungy and become a breeding ground for bacteria.
- If you don't have a dishwasher, make sure that you use hot soapy water to wash up all your pots and pans. You can get some snazzy washing-up gloves if you find the water too hot.
- Keep cooked and raw food separate – in the fridge and on surfaces while you are cooking.
- Use separate chopping boards for meat, fish and vegetables to avoid cross-contamination. You can buy a set of different coloured plastic ones quite cheaply.
- Never leave food out to defrost on a kitchen surface – check the defrosting instructions and follow them instead.
- Make sure that food you are freezing or putting in the fridge has completely cooled down first.
- To avoid food going off, keep your fridge at lower than 5°C.
- Empty the bin regularly and keep it free of dirt and mould.

> ⓘ **Need to know...**
> If you want to know more about food hygiene, check out **www.nhs.uk/Livewell/homehygiene/Pages/Homehygienehub.aspx** for tips and info on keeping your food safe in the kitchen.

Simple student recipes

📖 **The inside story: Cooking my first meal away from home**

Yes, I confess, it was out of a packet. It was pasta in sauce! Just add milk and water. I don't eat much of that kind of food now, but when I was a first-year student that was the first thing I reached for. But as I saw what others were eating and I read more and generally grew up, I saw that what I was eating wasn't good for me, plus I could make something much tastier and healthier in the same amount of time (10–12 minutes). After a semester I made mushrooms and cheese on toast. This took about 10 minutes, but at least it had fresh vegetables as a component. The pattern of that first recipe set me up for the next three years. I always tried to have vegetables as part of my meal and took fruit with me during the day to eat as a snack.

😀 **Inside tip**

'When I started uni I was so rubbish at cooking, I burnt everything! I got better by practising though. Don't give up if it goes wrong first time, keep on trying and you'll get there.'

Alex, 20, Carlisle

The overall price for each recipe will vary depending on where you are picking up the ingredients – shopping in cheaper shops will result in cheaper food bills, so bear that in mind when trying out these recipes.

That's not to say that you can't mix and match cheaper and more expensive items when shopping if you want. For example, you can buy some organic items like meat and then some non-organic bread, rice and staples, especially if you have specific dietary needs or you prefer eating organic foods.

Cheesy mushroom and ham omelette

Very cheap and simple to make.
Serves 1 hungry student.

Tools

- Saucepan
- Spatula
- Mug
- Knife and chopping board
- Frying pan (non-stick is crucial)
- Cheese grater

Grab

- 1 tablespoon margarine or oil
- 2 small mushrooms, sliced
- 2 eggs
- Slice of ham
- Handful of cheese, grated
- Salt and pepper to taste

Change it up – try combinations like spring onions and bacon, onion and cheese or tomato and basil

Now

1 Heat the margarine or oil until melted and bubbling. Fry the mushrooms until soft and set aside.
2 Crack the eggs into a mug and beat. Then pour the eggs into the pan and cook until almost set.
3 Tear the ham up into small pieces and add with the mushrooms and grated cheese to one half of the omelette.
4 Fold the 'empty' half over the 'filled' half of the omelette and let it cook for a few minutes. Season to taste and serve hot.

Sausage bake

Cheap and tasty.
Serves 4 hungry students.

Tools

- Saucepan
- Frying pan
- Ovenproof dish
- Kettle
- Spatula
- Knife and chopping board
- Colander
- Cheese grater

Grab

- 1 teaspoon margarine
- Pack of 8 sausages
- 4 handfuls pasta shapes
- 1 teaspoon mixed herbs
- 1 tablespoon tomato ketchup
- Salt and pepper
- Cheese, grated

Now

1 Heat margarine in frying pan until it becomes liquid, then add the sausages.

2 Turn the sausages frequently so that they are cooked evenly.

3 Pour boiling water into the saucepan and add the pasta. Let it boil for 3 minutes, then turn the heat down to simmering for a further 3 minutes.

4 When the pasta is cooked, drain and place in an ovenproof dish. Stir in ketchup and herbs. Season to taste with salt and pepper.

5 Chop the sausages up and add to the pasta in the dish. Stir and top with lots of grated cheese.

6 Bake in the oven at 200°C, Gas Mark 6, for 15–20 minutes until the cheese is golden brown and serve hot.

Easy sharing fajitas

Sharing the cost of the ingredients makes these fajitas fast to make and easy on the pocket. Alternatively, grab a fajita kit, add 500g of chicken and you can make fajitas for eight – great for parties and hangouts.

This recipe is meant to be a bit messy, so don't worry if stuff falls out of the fajita when you tuck in – it's all about the experience!

Serves four to six hungry students.

Tools

🍴 Large frying pan
🍴 Chopping board and knife

🍴 Grill or microwave

Grab

🍲 Meat, tofu or veggies of your choice (if you are using meat about 450–500g is enough for 6–8 people)
🍲 Oil or margarine
🍲 1 green pepper
🍲 Lettuce

🍲 Tomatoes
🍲 Plain flour tortillas – as many as you need
🍲 Sour cream
🍲 Salsa
🍲 Garlic salt and white/black pepper to season chicken

N.B. Ingredients can be chosen per fajita, for example 1 tomato, 2 lettuce leaves, a handful of meat, vegetables or tofu per person; I buy a whole lettuce, a pack of tomatoes and a pack of frozen meat, then use what I need and save the rest

Change it up – add spicy mince mixed with tinned tomatoes to your tortilla instead

Now

1 Start by frying the chopped meat, tofu or vegetables in margarine or oil in a frying pan.
2 Roughly chop the green pepper and add to the meat, tofu or vegetables.
3 Slice the tomatoes and tear the lettuce into strips.
4 Heat the tortillas under the grill or in the microwave for about 10 seconds – sprinkle with a few drops of water to stop them drying out.
5 When the meat, tofu or vegetables are cooked through, lay on the tortilla.
6 Add the chopped lettuce and tomatoes, laying them on top of the meat, tofu or vegetables. Season with salt and pepper to taste.
7 Spoon on salsa and sour cream according to taste.
8 Wrap up and go!

Puff pastry pizza

Easy to make, non-expensive, customisable and looks good too!
Serves up to 6 hungry students.

Tools

- Baking trays
- Kitchen foil
- Greaseproof paper
- Chopping board and knife
- Cheese grater

Grab

- 6 cherry tomatoes
- 1 small red onion, peeled and sliced
- Handful of sliced cooked chicken or any other meat you fancy
- 1 tablespoon olive oil
- 1 pack of puff pastry sheets – Jus-Rol, for example
- 1 tablespoon tomato ketchup
- Tomato purée
- 1 beaten egg
- Mozzarella or cheese

Change it up – add pepperoni, mushrooms and cooked peppers for a spicy version

> **Inside tip**
>
> 'If you're making messy food, make sure you always have kitchen roll handy. You can mop up spills and chuck it all in the bin – no minging tea towels to wash!'
>
> *Rob, 19, Essex*

Now

1. Pre-heat the oven to 200°C, Gas mark 6.
2. Put the red onion, tomatoes and cooked chicken on a baking tray lined with kitchen foil, drizzle with a tablespoon of olive oil and roast in the oven until soft.
3. Place a sheet of puff pastry onto a floured surface. Roll up the edges so that the sheet forms a rectangle with a raised border. Smear with tomato purée and tomato ketchup and brush with the beaten egg.

4 Lay the pastry on a fresh baking tray lined with greaseproof paper.

5 Add the onion, tomatoes and chicken. Top with torn mozzarella or grated cheese.

6 Bake for 15 minutes or until the pastry is golden brown. Allow to cool, then slice and serve.

'You choose' stir-fry

Cost depends on ingredients – veggie cheaper than meat, for example.

Serves 2 hungry students – for 1 hungry student make with half of each ingredient.

I call this the 'You choose' stir-fry because you can add or change pretty much anything! Eat with chopsticks – very impressive once you've learnt how to use them!

Tools

- Saucepan
- Wok
- Wooden spoon
- Chopping board and knife

Grab

- Noodles, 1 layer per person
- 1 tablespoon sesame or sunflower oil
- Meat (chicken or beef) or tofu, sliced, or prawns
- 2 cloves garlic, minced
- 4 spring onions, sliced
- 1 green pepper, sliced
- 1 pack stir-fry vegetables (less than £1 in most supermarkets)
- Dark soy sauce
- Sweet chilli sauce or a sauce of your choice to drizzle over

Change it up – use rice instead of noodles; brown rice is healthiest

Now

1 Cook the noodles in boiling salted water as directed on the pack.
2 Add a tablespoon of oil to the wok.
3 Toss the sliced meat or tofu, garlic, spring onions and green pepper in the oil. Stir fry for 4 minutes, making sure that the meat is cooked inside.
4 Add the stir-fry vegetables, prawns if you're using them, cooked and drained noodles and a splash of soy sauce. Stir-fry for about 5 minutes.
5 Add your choice of sauce and let sit for 1 minute – then feast!

3 veg mash

Inexpensive.   Serves 2 hungry students.

I stumbled on this when deciding between sweet potatoes or Maris Pipers to use in my mash one evening. This recipe is a great side dish with meat, tofu, vegetables or fish and you're also getting some of your five a day! It tastes amazing with grilled lamb chops and mango chutney on top.

Tools:

- Large bowl or dish
- Potato masher
- Wooden spoon or spatula
- Colander
- 3-tier steamer or large pan
- Chopping board and knife

Grab

- 2 sweet potatoes, peeled and cubed
- 2 potatoes, peeled and cubed
- 3 carrots, peeled or scraped and chopped
- 1 tablespoon butter or margarine
- Milk
- Salt and black pepper to taste
- Mixed herbs

Change it up – replace the sweet potatoes with half a butternut squash, add garlic puree to give a zingy kick

Now

1 Boil or steam the chopped vegetables, until you can run a knife smoothly through each type.
2 Strain and put into a large dish. Add the butter or margarine.
3 Mash until it's the consistency you like. Add a splash of milk if it's too stiff.
4 Add mixed herbs and salt and pepper to taste.

Gourmet toast

Cheaper than chips! The ultimate easy, quick and filling snack.
You can customise it with pretty much whatever's in the fridge.
Try combinations like tomato and cheddar, red onion and cheddar or pepperoni and mozzarella.

Serves 1 hungry student.

Tools

- Grill
- Frying pan
- Chopping board and knife
- Cheese grater

Grab

- Bread, 2 slices
- 1 teaspoon butter or margarine
- 4 mushrooms, chopped
- A handful of grated cheese
- Black pepper

💬 Inside tip

'In the winter our flat was freezing, so we warmed our plates or bowls in the bottom of the oven while we cooked dinner on the hob. When we'd finished cooking the plates were nice and toasty and the food didn't go cold. Make sure you use oven gloves to take the plates out, though!'

Charlie, 20, Edinburgh

Now

1 Turn the grill to a medium heat and lightly toast two slices of bread.
2 Melt a teaspoon of butter or margarine in a frying pan over a medium heat. Fry the mushrooms until soft.
3 Scatter the grated cheese on the toasted bread and pop back under the grill on a low heat.
4 When the cheese is golden brown, place the mushrooms on top.
5 Sprinkle with black pepper and eat while warm.

Spicy carrot and coriander soup

Buy the vegetables in bulk to keep the cost down and this recipe will be surprisingly cheap.

Serves 1 hungry student with about 6 servings to spare – freeze and enjoy again another time.

Tools

- Large heavy-based saucepan
- Wooden spoon
- Chopping board and knife
- Blender

Grab

- 1 tablespoon vegetable oil
- 1 large onion, peeled and chopped
- 6 carrots, peeled or scraped and chopped
- 2 potatoes, peeled and chopped
- 1 handful or pack of fresh coriander
- 2 cloves of garlic, minced
- Half a pint of stock – I dissolve 2 vegetable stock cubes in half a pint of boiled water
- 1 tablespoon mixed herbs
- Salt and pepper to taste – garlic salt makes the soup extra tasty

Change it up – add 4 potatoes and a large red onion instead of the coriander to make a thick, hearty soup

Now

1 Heat the oil in the pan on a medium heat. Add the onion and fry until soft.
2 Add the carrots, potatoes and stock. Turn up the heat and boil for 20 minutes. Pop the lid on and cook down until you can pierce the vegetables with a knife smoothly.
3 Put the coriander into the blender and pour in the contents of the pan. Blend until smooth and then add salt and pepper to taste. Hot pepper sauce adds a bit of a kick – just a dash will do.

Simple lasagne

Serves 1 hungry student with about 5 servings to spare.

For a vegetarian option replace the meat with Quorn or a thick vegetable like aubergine, sliced lengthways, or sliced tomatoes. For a vegan option, replace the meat with tofu or a handful of frozen spinach and use vegan-friendly lasagne sheets and cheese substitute.

Tools

- Rectangular lasagne dish
- Medium-sized pan
- Wooden spoon or spatula
- Chopping board and knife

Grab

- 1 tablespoon butter or oil
- 1 onion, peeled and chopped

- 3 garlic cloves, chopped finely
- 500g or three handfuls of frozen minced meat (normally beef)
- Salt and pepper to taste
- 1 tablespoon mixed herbs
- Handful mushrooms, sliced – optional
- Tinned or fresh tomatoes, chopped
- 1 carrot, peeled or scraped and grated
- Red sauce (see later recipe)
- Egg pasta lasagne sheets – about 9 sheets for three layers
- White sauce (see later recipe)
- Mozzarella or cheddar cheese

Change it up – the more veggies the better! Try adding cauliflower and courgette for a richer taste

Now

1 Preheat the oven to 200°C, Gas Mark 6.
2 Heat butter or oil in a pan over a low heat and add the onion and garlic.
3 When the onion and garlic are soft, add the frozen or fresh minced meat.
4 When the meat has browned, add, salt, pepper and mixed herbs.
5 Add the mushrooms, tomatoes and carrots to the pan and mix well.
6 Add the red sauce and stir well.
7 Put a lid on the pan and simmer over a low heat for five minutes.
8 Pour a third of this sauce into the lasagne dish, layer lasagne sheets over to cover all the contents, then layer a third of the white sauce on top of that.
9 Repeat step 8 twice more and then scatter grated cheese or mozzarella on top of all that. (The size of your dish and the thickness of the layers you prefer may vary, so learn as you go what works best for you.)
10 Cook in the oven for 30–40 minutes until golden brown.
11 Serve!

White sauce

It's really easy to make white sauce. You can also add cheese and stir in cooked macaroni to make macaroni cheese. You can't leave the stove when making this sauce otherwise it could burn!

Tools

- Whisk (a plastic or metal 'balloon' whisk is best)
- Medium non-stick saucepan
- Wooden spoon

Grab

- 2 tablespoons butter
- 2 tablespoons flour
- Mug (250ml) of cold milk
- Salt and pepper to taste

Now

1 Melt the butter in the pan over a medium heat until it is completely liquid.
2 Add the flour bit by bit, stirring as you go.
3 What you are aiming for is a stiff paste, known as a roux.
4 Add half the milk slowly, stirring all the while.
5 Now whisk in the rest of the milk slowly.
6 Whisk the sauce vigorously until it is smooth without lumps. Add salt and pepper to taste.

Red sauce

This is the sauce I use as a base for bolognaise and lasagne. Halve the quantities for 1 hungry student or make it and save half for a spaghetti bolognaise later in the week.

To make bolognaise: Brown 200g of minced meat, a small chopped onion and a handful of chopped mushrooms in 1 tablespoon of oil over a medium heat. Add the sauce and cook for 20 minutes. Boil half a handful of spaghetti in salted water until soft. Pour the sauce over the cooked spaghetti and tuck in.

Tools

- ⚑ Wooden spoon
- ⚑ Large saucepan
- ⚑ Chopping board and knife

Grab

- 1 teaspoon margarine
- 1 small onion, chopped
- 2 garlic cloves, crushed
- 2 tomatoes, chopped
- 2 teaspoons mixed herbs
- Salt and pepper to taste
- 1 tablespoon tomato ketchup

Now

1 Melt the margarine in the pan over a low heat and cook the onions and garlic until soft.
2 Add the tomatoes and mixed herbs.
3 Simmer with the lid on for about 20 minutes, until the ingredients have become liquid.
4 Stir in the ketchup and salt and pepper to taste.

The ultimate easy cake

I've made this simple Victoria sponge many times – and it's yummy!

Tools

- Wooden spoon – if you want to be hardcore
- Electric mixer – if you want it done quickly!
- Mixing bowl
- Spatula
- Two 10-inch cake tins
- Greaseproof paper
- Wire cooling rack

Grab

- Cake mix:
- 6oz/175g butter or margarine
- 6oz/175g caster sugar (granulated sugar will also work)
- 3 eggs
- 1 teaspoon vanilla essence
- 6oz/175g self-raising flour
- For the buttercream filling:
- 3oz/85g butter or margarine
- 6oz/175g icing sugar
- 2 tablespoons jam – strawberry or raspberry works best

Change it up – add 2 tablespoons cocoa powder to the cake mix and a large melted chocolate bar to the buttercream filling and you make a yummy chocolate cake. Add the zest of two lemons to the cake mix and the juice of half a lemon to the buttercream to make a lemon sponge cake

Now

1 Heat the oven to 180°C, Gas mark 4. Smear a teaspoon of butter around the tins and line them with greaseproof paper.

2   Cream (stir briskly) the butter and sugar together with the wooden spoon until the mixture looks light and fluffy. Major elbow grease is needed here – or use an electric mixer on medium speed.
3   Stir in the beaten eggs in three stages, mixing well between each addition. Add the vanilla essence and stir in. Sift in the flour and stir gently.
4   Split the mixture between the two greased tins. Bake for about 25 minutes, without opening the oven door.
5   Take the cakes out and turn out of the tins onto a wire rack to cool.
6   Wash up the mixing bowl and reuse it to make the buttercream filling.
7   For the filling, beat the butter with a wooden spoon or electric whisk until it's smooth and creamy. Sift in the icing sugar in four stages, mixing well between each addition.
8   Now spread the flat side of one of the cooled cakes with a thick layer of jam, spread the other with the buttercream filling and squish together.
9   Add candles for a celebration and you're done!

Food and eating are a very important part of life, but especially at university. If you don't get it right you'll miss out on having a healthy body and a healthy pocket. Eat in moderation and don't be afraid to try new things.

I've put in these recipes as guidelines, but you can customise the ingredients and make them your own. Have fun learning!

Student to Student to Student

5
Study

When it comes to exams and assignments, try not to worry or get too stressed. They've got to be done and you will be able to do them. The change in standard of work from A-level to university will take some getting used to, so don't feel like you should know exactly what to do straight away.

Universities have specific referencing systems, research methods and academic writing styles. But don't panic about these, because there is always help available through the academic advisers and extra training at your university.

I've recommended quite a few study books in this chapter to help you get stuck in, as well as offering tips and encouragement to keep you afloat. Keep positive and enjoy learning new things!

Study tips and insights

- ✍ Save your work *as you go* – not at the end of the essay. If your computer crashes or loses power supply, or you hit the wrong button, you could lose all the work you have done. It's good to back everything up on a dedicated USB stick as well.

- ✪ Make sure that your laptop is fully charged if you are going to be working away from a plug socket. There's nothing worse than it dying when you haven't got a spare battery or power source.
- ✪ Keep a spare pair of headphones in your laptop sleeve or bag for study moments.
- ✪ Keep a simple study schedule and write an essay plan before you start. This helps you to be sure that everything that needs to be read or included is done and dusted.
- ✪ Speak with your lecturer or tutor and ask questions if you aren't sure what you are meant to do for an assignment. If you're confused, there are probably others who feel the same way too, so everyone benefits.
- ✪ Don't leave your assignment until the day before it's due – this equals panic and a lot of stress that you can easily avoid.
- ✪ Try not to revise for an exam before you go to bed. Relax instead. Revise in the daytime when you're more alert and more likely to remember what you're studying.
- ✪ Don't lock yourself away and become a study hermit. Carry on with your usual activities and plan your study time around them.
- ✪ Use your module style guide to make sure that you have your referencing, bibliography and presentation spot on and also to avoid losing extra marks.
- ✪ Always look back at your essay plan if you feel you are rambling.
- ✪ Do refer back to your lecture notes to add more meat to your essay.
- ✪ Do think about what you are really trying to say.
- ✪ Don't try to impress the marker with jargon. If you can say it simply, then do so.
- ✪ Do read your work aloud, a few times, to check that it makes sense and flows naturally.
- ✪ Don't forget to check your spelling by eye as well as using a word-processing spell checker. A spell check won't pick up the difference between their and there, for example.
- ✪ If there's an emergency or crisis that's preventing you from finishing by the given deadline, ask your lecturer for an extension.

⤴ Try your best, and don't be intimidated by other students' grades and comments. If anything, let competition spur you on to achieve the best grades you can.

⤴ Do celebrate when you achieve well and don't let disappointment outweigh your best efforts.

⤴ Love your subject. If you feel that you don't know enough, take a few books out at the library and fill yourself full of information.

Making a study schedule

Making a study schedule breaks that mountain of work down into manageable chunks that will be less intimidating and more inviting. I find the best time to use a study schedule or plan is when you have a reading week, so you can read ahead, study and catch up on work you may be behind with.

Keep your study schedule simple. If it gets too complicated you won't be able to read it, let alone follow it successfully. I use a large whiteboard so I can erase what I've covered as I go. Some students like to use a paper or electronic version.

The first thing to do is note down all your deadlines. I put a red box around the day the assignment is due and then a red star at the start of the week before, to remind myself that I've only got a few days before I have to hand something in.

Write out your schedule as a 'to do' list. Then add anything else you need to do or catch up on as you go along. Maybe you need to use the days of the week as your guideline, for example Monday revise American Literature, Tuesday test self on American Literature and start going over Colonial History, and so on. Split each day up and try to spend an hour or so on each assignment. That way it won't all come as a massive shock when you have a day left.

We've all left work until the last minute for one reason or another. Here are some emergency tips to help you feel a bit less nervous if you do get into a fix:

1 Don't put the problem off or ignore your deadline.

2 Don't despair, there's always something you can do.

3 Do speak to your lecturer and ask if you can have an extension.

4 Don't try to rush through it – if you have time, still get your work checked at your study skills centre for last-minute mistakes.

5 Do learn from your mistakes – try not to repeat the same one.

With a study schedule you can see how much time you are actually spending on studying. Quite a few of the students I spoke to say that they tend to make a flexible plan, so that if they do need to go somewhere the work they were going to cover doesn't get missed out.

Do what works best for you. Some days you will be able to study for an hour straight and some days you may only be able to get in 10–15-minute slots. Be flexible and work with your life.

> **☺ Inside tip**
>
> 'I find an empty classroom at university and study in there. I prefer it because I like to spread all my books and stuff out while I work. There are loads of empty classrooms at my university so it's never a problem.'
>
> *Emily, 24, Bath*

To-do lists

It's easy to forget things. Students have so much to do – work, assignments, social life, bills, the list goes on. I normally start the day by writing a list, which helps me to prioritise what I need to do. For example, a daily list while you're at university may look like this:

- ↻ Start planning American Literature essay.
- ↻ Confirm office hours with Sarah.
- ↻ Return books.
- ↻ Book Glasto tickets.

Nowhere on that list do I mention Facebook, but it does happen, doesn't it? We all deviate and watch a movie online or check out videos on YouTube; it's inevitable. But making a list can help you keep on track. Even if you look at it at the end of the day after you get caught up in other stuff, there are still things you can get done.

Retaining information in lectures

My lectures were one to two hours long. If we'd been expected to remember everything the lecturer said for that time it would be a horrendous task. Thank goodness it's not like that. Lectures are often split into talking *and* interaction, so you're not listening to one person speak for 120 minutes without a break.

PowerPoint® slides and handout sheets are often used to help break up the information and appeal to different learning styles. You are normally allowed to take notes on your laptop and even record lectures and seminars – ask before you get out your recording device or smartphone just to make sure.

Here are some tips for making the most out of lectures:

- Use a notebook or lined A4 paper for notes to keep them neat.
- If you do take notes by hand, file them in folders to keep them from becoming disorganised.
- Keep the handouts together with the notes from that lesson and write the date on everything. This makes the notes easier to refer to when writing essays.
- Try not to be late to lectures, as it is really distracting for other people. If you are late, see if you can enter during the break.
- If you're not sure about something or want to know the source of particular information, ask about it.

Inside tip

'After some lectures people would leave their handouts behind on the desk – I felt this was such a waste of time and money, not just for the lecturer who had prepared it, but the students themselves too.'

Sabina, 20, London

Inside tip

'Always bring paper and two pens – if your laptop battery dies during a lecture you have back-up.'

Tanika, 19, Sunderland

🖎 Read the prior reading ahead of the lecture.

🖎 Try not to talk too much, as it can be off-putting for other people.

🖎 Sit where you can hear the lecturer.

Different note-taking techniques work for different students. Some find it easier to record a lecture and make notes afterwards, others like to take notes with pen and paper or a laptop. Whichever way you find best – do it!

Your teachers

Lecturers, seminar leaders and peer mentors are all there to help you through your time at university. If pressure from assignments is getting to you, have a chat with them. During your degree you'll have specific times and even a specific lesson in which you'll be able to ask your lecturer about the work you have to do. Make sure to use these times to get the information you need. Also, if you suspect that you have a learning difficulty, such as dyslexia, you should speak to your personal tutor or supervisor immediately. They will be able to advise you on how to go about getting the support you need.

Library staff

Library staff can really be a great help. They are trained in the secret ins and outs of the library and always seem to know where that important 'lost' book could be.

Don't feel worried about approaching library assistants; often they will have extra information that will help you save time in the long run. Ask them to recommend books on your subject – it beats trawling through every shelf trying to find something relevant!

It's important to know that the library system in a university may be different from the one in your local library. The cataloguing system at university normally follows the Dewey Decimal System and the books are in their decimal order, so for example 303.01/LOWELL would come before 303.1/LOWELL. If that doesn't make sense, ask an assistant to show you how the system works. You need to put books back on the shelves according to this way of organising too.

Reading lists and reserving items

Reading lists normally come out a few weeks before you are due to start a particular module. My advice is to get the books and read them in advance, not while the module is going on. With activities, socialising and the other assignments you will have, there simply isn't time for even more reading.

If you need a few books for an assignment, don't turn up at the library two days before the assignment is due and try to reserve them. More often than not some canny student has already reserved the book on a four-week loan, so you won't be able to use it for a while. It's best to get them in advance.

You can also check your university's online library catalogue to see if a book's on loan or on the shelf before you leave home.

Plagiarism and self-plagiarism

Plagiarism is using another person's idea or work and claiming that it's your own. If you are caught plagiarising it can lead to very serious results – you can be asked to leave your course and the university. It's the same with self-plagiarism, reusing your own work that's already been marked at your university.

Cutting, copying and pasting straight from the internet is only the tip of the iceberg when it comes to plagiarism. It can be tempting to 'reword' research you find online. I've been there myself, in the depths of despair over not having enough references or faced with the inevitable essay question that ends in *discuss*. The bottom line is – don't panic. Think hard enough and you *can* do it.

Some students do reword what they find or copy other essays. But with all the technology used in universities to check students' work for plagiarism, there isn't any point in chancing it. Instead of cheating, use what you're paying for – what you're being taught and what you're researching. Plagiarism and self-plagiarism aren't smart and won't get you anywhere.

However, if you do plagiarise or even self-plagiarise and it's a genuine mistake, explain this to your lecturer as soon as you notice what you have done – the sooner the better, to avoid unnecessary questioning.

ⓘ Need to know...

One of the many books I use when I'm writing essays is called *Referencing and Understanding Plagiarism* (2009), by Kate Williams and Jude Carroll, published by Palgrave Macmillan. It's pocket sized and covers everything you need to produce a plagiarism-free assignment.

Using the internet

The internet is a useful tool for studying, when used properly. Here are some guidelines for making the internet work for you when studying:

- ☙ Bookmark the pages you find useful and assign these bookmarks to a separate folder on your desktop marked 'Study'.
- ☙ If a site looks dodgy, don't use it. Always try to establish who wrote the information you're using and what their credentials are.
- ☙ If you're feeling stuck, ask your tutor for recommended study websites or particular sites for your subject.
- ☙ If you need help with a topic, type it into a search engine or your online library catalogue to find more material that could help.

Terminology

Each degree subject has its own 'language'. For example, if someone said 'tort' I would immediately think of some kind of chocolate-covered cake, a 'torte', but to a law student tort is a type of law. That's why it's important to read ahead. Then you'll know the language your assignments are meant to be written in.

If you get stuck on a particular piece of jargon, have a look through your module guides or drop an email to your lecturer or tutor. Even better, get to know someone on the year above so that they can fill you in on all the lingo.

Grammar and spelling

Isn't it annoying when that squiggly red line appears under a word in your assignment while you're typing and you don't know whether it's right or wrong? Even more so when you write form instead of from and it doesn't get picked up at all? That's why it's important to let someone you trust read your work. Take your assignment to the study skills centre – even if you think it's perfect, it's guaranteed that someone else will always see what you can't.

You can lose and gain marks based on your spelling and grammar, so make sure that you check your work thoroughly before you hand it in and use extra eyes if you can. A paper or online dictionary is always handy for words with both English and American spellings.

> ## ⓘ Need to know...
>
> See if your university has skills4studycampus, described as the 'interactive e-learning resource for students'. This software is brilliant for developing the four main study skills:
>
> - Writing
> - Reading and note-taking
> - Referencing and avoiding plagiarism
> - Critical thinking
>
> There are audio guides to listen to and tests to see how you're getting on. If you're missing out, email the link below (after checking it out yourself) to your librarian and see if they can install it for you and the rest of the student body:
>
> www.palgrave.com/ skills4studycampus/ skills4studyScrubWeb.html

Before you hand in any work for marking, make sure that you have followed what I like to call **W**hite **C**ats **R**eally **B**e **P**artying, **N**orman

- ꙮ **W**ord **C**ount
- ꙮ **R**eferencing
- ꙮ **B**ibliography
- ꙮ **P**age **N**umbers

I know it's a silly sentence, but it helped me remember to check all of the above. You can definitely lose marks for missing an element like a bibliography, or going under or over the word count you're allowed. Perhaps write down the sentence on a Post-it® note to help you remember what to check before hitting the Send button.

Study buddy

Studying alongside another person or in a public place can have a positive effect, rather than the negativity of being a 'study hermit'. We all need time to ourselves to study, but don't make it such a habit that you don't come out of your room at all. You may learn something new while you're studying with other people. Whether it's a communal library desk or beanbags on the floor, share your space and time and try to learn together.

> 💬 **Inside tip**
>
> **'If you don't know what to do for an assignment, definitely ask one of the people in your class and see if you can help each other.'**
>
> *Dave, 19, Carlisle*

Remember back in school when you would whisper and ask the person next to you how to do something, then get into trouble for talking? University isn't like that. Most lecturers encourage students to work with the person sitting next to them and plan presentations together. Take working with others as an opportunity to learn something new and get to know people better.

Don't despise an hour

Even though 60 minutes seems a short time, you can actually get a lot done. I once got 3500 words written in an hour. Granted, it wasn't word perfect and I went back and edited it later, but it's a start, and sometimes with an essay that's all you need.

The ability to 'get it all down' then come back to it later is one I have had to learn. I remember in my first year I would try and try to write everything perfectly the first time. The more I learnt in my years at university, the more I saw that the way other people did it wasn't working for me. You'll learn the best way for you through trial and error.

Grade boundaries

Most universities follow these guidelines for allocating grades:

First 70%+
2:1 60–69%
2:2 50–59%
Third 40–49%
Fail less than 40%

> 💬 **Inside tip**
>
> 'When you get your assignments back, look at the mark and tutor's comments – the comments help you understand what you did well and what you can improve.'
>
> *Clare, 20, Middlesex*

If you want to stay at a healthy average, then really it all comes down to the amount of time you put into your work. Don't get me wrong – I knew of some students who could churn out an amazing essay the night before the deadline. But you want to aim for the best. Who knows how much better you could have done if you had given yourself more time?

It's also important to know that each lecturer has different quirks and requests. They may like work presented with headings for the introduction, main body and conclusion, or they may not. They will explain and let you know before setting your assignment if they have any particular issues with presentation, but if in doubt ask.

I know what it's like to leave work to pile up and then cram at the last minute –it's really hard to deal with it all. Save yourself the stress and get started early. Sometimes you will have to forgo that cinema or shopping trip to catch up on pending work. Don't feel like you're alone in this. Every student at some point will feel the stress caused by deadlines. Talk with your friends about it and even work together in the same room.

> ### 💬 Inside tip
>
> **'If you are using a laptop or PC while you're studying, remember to take frequent breaks to give your eyes a rest. Every 20–30 minutes works well for me. If you don't take regular breaks then you may end up with a headache or eye strain. I set a timer on my phone so I don't forget.'**
>
> *Shevaughn, 27, York*

> ### 💬 Inside tip
>
> **'I'm dyslexic and find it harder than most to navigate and digest books in general. I always go to the support staff for help and watch videos. I'm more of a visual learner. A good website I used was www.beingdyslexic. co.uk, it's got useful study methods that actually work and a lot of information on dyslexia too – check it out.'**
>
> *Katie, 19, East Anglia*

Key study skills books

I've searched around for the top study books and give short reviews of them here. These choices are based on what I have found successful as an academic adviser, library recommendations, student recommendations and reviews from the most popular bookselling sites. If you're not sure, check them out at the library first and see which ones work best for you.

The Study Skills Handbook, 3rd edn (2008), by Stella Cottrell, published by Palgrave Macmillan.

This book is well designed and easy to use. It covers everything you need and is written in a friendly, open way. You can dip in and out of it when you need to. Definitely a good investment that can be used throughout your degree.

How to Write Better Essays, 2nd edn (2008), by Bryan Greetham, published by Palgrave Macmillan.

When I'm advising a student I tend to have this book open on the desk. If you're looking for help with essay structure or how to develop your argument, this is the book to get.

Critical Thinking Skills: Developing Effective Analysis and Argument, 2nd edn (2011), by Stella Cottrell, published by Palgrave Macmillan.

This informative book will help you to get ahead of the crowd and make your work effective. It's not until you've worked your way through the book that you see how much more you can get out of your assignments. When you see the word 'analyse' in an essay question, does your mind automatically go blank? This book teaches you, in a clear and straight-to-the-point way, how to analyse texts and arguments properly.

Cite Them Right: The Essential Referencing Guide, 8th edn (2010), by Richard Pears and Graham Shields, published by Palgrave Macmillan.

Another book I have open on the table when advising students. Each university chooses to use a different style guide, sometimes different ones for different subjects. For some students Harvard referencing or MHRA (Modern Humanities Research Association) is standard, but there are other style guides too. This book will give you all the information you need.

Brilliant Writing Tips for Students (2009), by Julia Copus, published by Palgrave Macmillan.

This book is clear, straight to the point and easy to read – not to mention pocket sized. Great for revision on the move or to have open while you're studying.

***How to Write your Undergraduate Dissertation* (2009), by Bryan Greetham, published by Palgrave Macmillan.**

Greetham focuses on the undergraduate dissertation, while some of this book's competitors are a little vague as to whether their advice is aimed at postgraduate or undergraduate students. This book does what it says on the tin – with you in mind. If your dissertation is looming I would definitely say get a copy, even if it's just from the library. Have a read through before you start your dissertation so that you're well prepared.

***The Good Study Guide*, 2nd edn (2005), by Andy Northedge, published by The Open University.**

If you're nervous about studying, check this book out. It has tips on note taking, referencing and even time management. It's written in a clear, easy-to-read way and is produced by The Open University, noted for its successful course materials and academic books.

***The Ultimate Study Skills Handbook* (2010), by Sarah Moore, Colin Neville, Maura Murphy and Cornelia Connolly, published by Open University Press.**

This book is very easy to read and gives simple guidance. If you're just starting out, it may be a good choice. My opinion is you should get the more challenging books about study skills, so that they last for the whole three years of your degree, not just the first.

Tips for buying study books

- ⟳ Don't be daunted by the amount of text in a book – you don't have to read it all in one go.
- ⟳ Flip through a book at the library before you purchase it.
- ⟳ Find out if there is an electronic version of the book available. You may be able to download it onto your Kindle, smartphone or laptop to save on space.
- ⟳ Check your university bookshop for promotions and deals, as well as looking on bookselling sites such as www.amazon.co.uk and www.abebooks.com.
- ⟳ Browse through books at your leisure to see what's best for you and don't forget to check out the reviews.
- ⟳ Read the contents list to see if the book covers what you need.

꙳ You don't have to stick to books with the word 'study' on them. If there's a specific area you need help in, like reading or referencing, have a look at books that focus on that, too.

Are you stressed out?

Stress comes in many different forms. Sometimes you don't even know you're stressed until someone says you are, and then you get more stressed because you think everyone can tell! The first thing to do is come to terms with the fact that stress from exams and university is normal. You're not on your own at all.

☺ **Pocket money generator**

Can you create a study guide blog on your university website? You could review your top study books, gather student suggestions and even get paid by the human resources department. Make some enquiries and see what happens.

💬 **Inside tip**

'Log out of social networking, media and auction sites so that it's harder to get distracted – sometimes I also disable notifications from my phone.'

Mei, 22, Oxford

Signs of stress include headaches, being tense, fatigue and stomach upsets. If you are feeling this way, stop and look in the mirror. Say: 'I can do this and I will do the best I can – and that is good enough.' I know it sounds a bit cheesy, but you need to replace the negative with the positive. The more you do that, the less stressed you'll end up being.

Exams

You may be going to university thinking that exams will be really hard and scary, but really they're just like a spelling test – seeing what you remember and whether you can write it clearly and accurately. To think of them this way may not make much impact right now, but later down the line you'll see that exams are there to help you learn and get better at your subject.

Here's my advice for exam sanity.

Before

- ↻ Write down when and where your exam is and what it is on. Write it on your wall planner and in your academic planner so you can refer to it when you need to.
- ↻ Revise the work that's going to be covered in the exam and use prompt cards to help you remember. Look at past papers so you're sure of the form of the exam, and make notes on answering past questions as practice.
- ↻ Get together a pencil case with working pens, sharpened pencils and any other stationery or tools you need.
- ↻ Exercise helps relieve stress, so take part in your usual activities – don't stay inside worrying.
- ↻ Arrive early so that you're not too stressed.

During

- ↻ Make sure that your phone is switched off – even vibrate makes a noise.
- ↻ Keep calm.
- ↻ If you see a question you don't have a clue about, leave it and come back to it later.
- ↻ Don't look around while you're sitting the exam.

> 💬 **Inside tip**
>
> 'Exams at A-level and exams in university really weren't that different. As long as you revise a bit each day up to the exam you'll be fine.'
>
> *Max, 22, Chester*

- ↻ Wear a watch so that you can keep track of the time without having to raise your head.
- ↻ Keep hydrated by bringing an unmarked water bottle with you.
- ↻ Make sure your handwriting stays neat.
- ↻ Read all the questions through very carefully and work out how much time you have to spend on each one, then stick to that timetable.

After

🕸 Don't forget to take your belongings with you.

🕸 Chatting about the exam sometimes makes the stress worse. It may work for you, but be aware that others may not want to discuss it, especially if they feel they could have done better.

🕸 Breathe a sigh of relief and await your results!

For further advice on taking exams, read *The Exam Skills Handbook*, 2nd edn (2011), by Stella Cottrell, published by Palgrave Macmillan.

> 😀 **Inside tip**
>
> 'To revise properly I actually had to leave the university. I went to this quiet bookshop I know with a café downstairs, because it had the main three things I need to study – food, drink and anonymity.
>
> *Rachel, 21, London*

Successful studying

To sum up:

🕸 Give yourself enough time to plan, write, edit and check your assignments properly.

🕸 Don't rely on a word-processing program to check your spelling; errors will still remain if your work is unchecked by the human eye.

🕸 Take notes and highlight pages as you read through long texts or books – being active like this stops processing large chunks of text from being boring, and makes it easier to find the points you found useful in the text.

🕸 Make wise choices about where you study. Coffee shops, libraries and your room are good places to get in the studying mood. It doesn't have to be your university library either. Why not try the British Library in London or a major library near you?

- Have your referencing and bibliography guidelines to hand. Even better, print out a full copy of your university style guide and refer to it while writing your assignment.
- Make sure that the font you use is clear and legible. The standard font is Arial or Times New Roman and the most widely accepted size is 12 point.
- Write a mini checklist of all the things every assignment needs, for example page numbers, your name, correct margins and justification.
- Have your subject handbook to hand and attend extracurricular lectures and workshops on presenting work properly. It all pays off in the end and you get value for money.
- If you do keep leaving it to the last minute to complete an assignment, bite the bullet and visit the study skills centre or read some of the books I've mentioned in this chapter.

Study is the part of being at university that really counts. Make what you are studying work for you and don't lose sight of your investment.

You learn how to be successful at studying, it doesn't come naturally. You're not expected to know how to study and produce work at university standard immediately. Use all the resources your university offers, read up on study skills and you'll have a big grin on your face when you hand in your assignments – on time, grammatically perfect and with arguments that are discussed clearly and passionately.

6

Managing, Making and Saving Money

With the cost of degrees hitting the roof it's hard for students to part with any money these days. It can be tough to get by, but money-saving tips, coupons and free stuff can help make university life much easier. Of course, having a job is an option that all students have to consider because the cost of living is very high.

I hope that this chapter will help you become even more finance savvy and get value for money out of your time at university — and some freebies along the way.

Managing your money

Once you know the amount of your student loan and/or grant, you need to look at your likely expenditure and work out how you're going to fit it all in. It's important to plan, because although you will probably have an overdraft available for those emergency bills, overspending or holiday security, it's best not to live on one if possible.

(i) Need to know...

Check out www.studentcalculator.org.uk. It's the best website I've found for working out your budget. It's easy to use and compares your entitlements, income and outgoings side by side. The site also has a international student calculator, so no one's left out!

Budget planning

ⓘ **Need to know...**

More of an 'on the go' person? Why not check out the Palgrave Macmillan *My Student Budget Planner* app for smartphones. It is easy to use and does all the hard work for you.

In my first semester of university I started out with a simple monthly in and out list to use as a budget, but after a while I found that it didn't always work out the way I'd planned! The amount I ended up spending varied as different situations came up. For example, I couldn't factor in an extra trip to see the family at the last minute, or my insurance going up, not to mention the small things like iTunes purchases or 'buy one, get one free' deals at the supermarket.

The best thing is to learn as you go. Try recording on paper what you spend each day, including your daily food consumption, coffees, travel – every little thing counts. By the second semester I'd done some research and printed out a simple spreadsheet, which I filled in by hand until I started seeing patterns in my outgoings. By the end of my first year I had moved on to a weekly budget planner, where I could factor in my income too and see how I was overspending.

For a kickstart, type 'student budget planner' into an internet search engine and have a look at the sites and links that come up. Make sure that you click on secure sites, the ones that look as if they're reputable. There are new budget planners being created all the time, so if one doesn't work check back and try another.

By the end of your first year things will have settled down financially and you'll see what you spend most of your money on. For me this was travel, food, going out and books for my courses. You may have a part-time job by then to give you more cash and be a complete pro at budgeting as well. It just takes practice.

Not spending too much

Here are a few tips to help you secure the best bargains:

- If you see something you like and it's not in short supply, wait – prices can go down from £75 to £25 within weeks. Ask the shop assistant and they may tell you when the next sale is.

- Try to go shopping in the morning before it's busy – shops like Primark may be cheap, but when they get busy I'd pay extra to get out!

- Compare online sales to store sales, especially for technological items. For example, some laptops or games are actually cheaper in the online sale than the bricks-and-mortar shop sale.

> 💬 **Inside tip**
> **'I saved money by catching the free intercampus bus or walking to and from the train station.'**
> *Agnieszka, 20, Kingston*

Online banking

Online banking is an easy way to keep track of your finances. Your statement is accessible 24 hours a day so you can see what's happening in your account. You can also make transfers as you need or set up a new savings account.

Direct debits and standing orders are particularly important to keep up with. It sucks when you don't have enough money in your account and you get a charge from the bank for an unpaid item. Also, if a direct debit isn't paid it can leave a note on your credit rating that makes it difficult to get a loan later on, such as a career development loan.

Make sure to keep your personal banking and log-in details safe and secure at all times.

Career builder

Have you got into debt and needed help to get out of it? Could you use your personal experience with debt to help others avoid it and extract themselves from it? Maybe you could become a financial adviser at your university student advice centre.

Inside tip

'Use your smartphone to organise your money. Download your bank's app and then you can transfer money and see your spending on the go. Always use a passcode to protect your phone and sign out of the app when you're done.'

Paola, 22, Cambridge

Making money

To cover all those outgoings in your budget spreadsheet, you'll have to have an income. Surviving on your maintenance loan, maintenance grant and bursary is pretty optimistic. My friends all had jobs and I did too. Having a job, however small, is good for your university life. It's a change of scene, a good way to meet new people and a definite CV booster.

But working 9 to 5 is pretty much impossible while you are at university. With lectures, social events and societies, it's difficult to fit any kind of job in, but it is possible.

There's more on this in Chapter 7, but I can't stress enough how getting a job at university is a good idea in the long run – as long as the work-to-study ratio is balanced, you know the boundaries between the two and you let your boss know them too.

So here are some dos and don'ts of making money at university:

- ☙ Do remember that study is a priority over work.
- ☙ Don't commit to a job with a workload that you won't be able to fulfil.
- ☙ Do try to get a job that is close to your university and where you live. Travel costs add up.
- ☙ Don't forget to ask whether you can do more hours in the holidays.
- ☙ Do explore other options like paid reviewing (e.g. www.ciao.co.uk) and filling in surveys (e.g. www.valuedopinions.co.uk) to gain an extra bit of dosh.
- ☙ Do sell your clothes and other belongings on eBay before you buy more.
- ☙ Do remember that if someone offers you a chance to make money illegally, it will affect your life, and your standards, for ever. If you are caught you may lose your place at university, and possibly your freedom.
- ☙ Do use the skills you have. If you trained as a hairdresser, why not offer discounted cuts with a door-to-door service? That could be popular in halls. Or if you're good at cooking, why not offer some fun cooking classes?

> 💬 **Inside tip**
>
> 'I worked at the university to save time and money. I didn't get much pay for my job at the student bar, but what I didn't earn I made up for in tips and not having to pay travel costs.'
>
> *Kai, 19, Swansea*

Selling stuff

Can't shut your wardrobe door? It's time for a clear-out. Sort your clothes, shoes and accessories into piles. There may be groups for the charity shop, your friends, to keep and to throw away, but try to make a selling pile.

Selling your stuff online has never been easier, at auction sites like eBay or online classified ad sites like Gumtree. You can use your smartphone to photograph, list and collect money for your item. If you don't have a smartphone, as long as you can photograph your stuff auction websites are simple to use from your laptop. If you get stuck about what to say, have a look at a similar item to the one you are listing for another seller's approach.

Follow my ten golden rules for selling online:

1 Make sure that the condition you describe is the condition the item really is in. You don't want to disappoint a buyer, get bad feedback or even have to deal with a return and a refund because of an error on your part.

2 Write a good description of your item. Remember that you are *selling* it, so list all the attributes and why someone else might need it — and be positive, even when explaining faults.

3 If you are packaging something to post, try to recycle and cut down on extra packaging. If I was sending clothing I used to cut up a bin bag and wrap the item carefully with a label on the front — a roll of bin bags costs under 50p in some discount shops, so there can be big savings here. If you don't want to use bin liners, how about the padded envelopes you received your own post in? Save the envelopes, cut and stick paper over the whole front to disguise old addresses or postage, and there you go, a fresh envelope to use.

4 If you are selling on a site that lets you post photos of your item, make sure that the background is clear and that the item can be seen properly.

5 Agree payment options before you send anything, specifying in your listing whether you would accept a cheque or cash. I have found it best to buy and sell with PayPal, as although the fees can be offputting it is a safe and reliable way to send and receive your money.

6 Explore different selling sites to see which suits your goods best. Some, like www.etsy.com, let you specifically sell goods you have made; others, like www.amazon.co.uk, have rules about how much you can charge for postage for certain items, such as books and CDs.

7 Keep a record of how much you are making on each item to check that the effort is worthwhile.

8 Let your profits build up in your PayPal account, then use the money to buy Christmas and birthday presents.

9 Keep all your selling information in one place so that you don't get confused.

10 Keep your bank details and passwords safe and confidential at all times and sign out when you have finished using your selling website.

If you're not into online selling, or the seller fees that come with it, why not try doing a car boot sale? Take your stuff along and haggle away.

> 😊 **Pocket money generator**
>
> **Could you start up your own car boot sale? Hire a suitable field or school playground. Get the appropriate permission and staff. Charge sellers for tables and pitches – and start earning.**

Summer jobs

During the summer it may be hard to find a job, so make sure that you check out your local job centre. Depending on your circumstances, you may be entitled to claim jobseeker's allowance over the summer, so make sure that you drop in to the job centre when you finish each year to see if you can get some help. If you have a job before you leave for university, ask to be first on the list for extra hours over the summer and the usual holidays. But whatever you do, don't work too hard. There's more on balancing work, rest and social life in Chapter 8, Mind and Body.

Saving money

Food shopping

It's easy to get carried away when buying food. The best way to manage your food budget is to make a list of what you need and stick to it. I know that seems simple, but it works.

Online food shopping can also save you money. Because the temptations are on a screen rather than physically in front of you, it's easier to say no.

Set aside the amount of money you want to spend on food shopping, then do your shopping online, staying within the amount of money you have allocated. Make sure that you include any delivery charges as well. Online shopping may seem a bit fiddly at first, but it beats trekking back to your pad dragging three to four loaded shopping bags. Try www.mysupermarket.co.uk – not only does it show you the cheapest supermarket for what you're buying, it makes special offers much more obvious.

Another smart way to save money on food is by signing up to reward cards. Most supermarkets, restaurants and even coffee shops have some kind of incentive or loyalty card where you get points for every pound you spend in store or online. Points and coupons all add to the pennies in your pocket through future savings, so pick one up to save money.

> 💬 **Inside tip**
>
> 'I go to the supermarket at the end of the day to get ridiculously cheap veggies and other food – most items are discounted, so pop down and have a look.'
>
> *Mags, 24, Durham*

> 💬 **Inside tip**
>
> 'I saved up the points on my Tesco clubcard and took my mates to Alton Towers for free. If getting an amazing day out for free wasn't enough, I still had enough points to get a coupon towards my next shop.'
>
> *Kelly, 20, Bristol*

Storecards and discounts

A storecard is a little like a credit card. You put all your purchases on it then pay it off over time, or very quickly. But beware – although you often get a discount or some kind of promotion when you open a storecard account, it's easy to get smacked with very high interest rates and then charges if you miss a payment.

The best approach is to wait until you need to buy a coat or some other large purchase, then put it on the card, get the discount and when your statement comes through, pay the whole amount off and cancel the card.

Loads of shops now give student discounts of up to 20 per cent on production of your NUS Extra card, so ask at the till or check out the list of participating companies at www.nus.org.uk/en/nus-extra/. Sometimes other shops will give a student discount but don't advertise it very clearly, so make sure that you do ask. The actual discount will be higher or lower depending on which shop you go to. Some shops even double their normal student discount at certain times of year – it's like they know when the student grant comes in!

Watch out for promotions and sign up to a discount forum like www.vouchercodes.co.uk, where you can keep an eye on current offers and discounts, particularly those for students.

> 💬 **Inside tip**
>
> **'Print out a list of the stores and sites that offer student discount and keep it somewhere you can see it.'**
>
> *Carmel, 22, Wolverhampton*

Saving on travel

You can get a young person's railcard by visiting www.16–25railcard.co.uk. Sometimes the site even offers the railcard for half price, so make sure that you keep checking to see when that is. At a third off the price of every journey you make, you'll get your money back in a journey or two, so it's well worth the investment. Think of all the festivals you can get to on the cheap! It also comes in handy for visiting friends and family.

Speaking of travel, don't forget about using the coach to visit family and friends. Although it takes a good while longer than going by train, if you book in advance you can get where you need to go for under a fiver! My friends and I used www.megabus.com and www.nationalexpress.com to get tickets. You do have to book well in advance though, to obtain a good discount. If you're going to a festival, there's also a massive hold in the coach that'll keep all your muddy backpacks, tents and wellies well away from your last clean pair of jeans!

Saving online

There's an amazing site called www.freecycle.org. As the name suggests, it's all about recycling things for free. For example, say you're moving out of halls and you need a new bed, because your old one at home is now too small. You can list your old bed on freecycle and pick up a 'new' one for free at the same time. You simply sign up to a group in your area and exchange and pick up stuff for free. Instead of adding to landfill, you're reducing it.

A good website for savings is www.groupon.co.uk. You sign up and get email alerts for half-price meals, cheap days out and even fish manicures! It's a great site to be on if you're strapped for cash but want to do something fun. Also check out sites like www.vouchercodes.co.uk and www.myvouchercodes. co.uk to find and print out money-saving coupons and vouchers. You can even get a Vouchercodes app for your smartphone that saves you the cost of printing – you simply show the screen with the relevant code to the shop assistant or waiter.

> ☺ **Inside tip**
>
> 'I always kept about £20 spare that was only for use if I needed to see family. It was tempting to spend it, but the thought of seeing my family more often helped me to set it aside each month.'
>
> *Shaun, 19, Edinburgh*

> ☺ **Inside tip**
>
> 'Check out www.studentbeans.com – really good site for student deals and discounts for students.'
>
> *Andy, 20, Macclesfield*

Signing up to a retail store's online newsletter often means that you get annoying emails, but sometimes they include big discount codes, so it's worth it in the end.

Savings accounts

It is possible to keep your student loan and grant in a savings account so that the funds can gain interest. I had a friend who saved their entire loan and earned about £300.

If that seems impossible, how about getting into the habit of putting money aside each time you get it? Even if it means saving only 10 per cent, that's a starting point. If you do this every month for three years, you could end up with quite a tidy amount of cash.

I hope this chapter has encouraged you to realise that it is possible to make and save money while you're at university – and not just from working. Use your university facilities and experience to help someone else and earn a few bob while you do.

The next chapter is about working, which is not all about gaining money. Read on to find out more...

7

Working

> I know that with so much study and socialising working isn't always an option at university, but it adds to your CV and you can gain extra cash. This straight-to-the point chapter is all about getting the best return out of the time you put in.

Students are in a large amount of debt as soon as they graduate. Due to the recent rise in undergraduate fees, they will owe at least £27,000 and that's just in tuition fee loans. Many students will have to get overdrafts and even credit cards – then there's the dilemma of funding a postgraduate degree if you want to carry on in higher education. As a result, many students now have to work part time while they study, just to limit the amount of money they have to pay back after they graduate.

The work/study balance

First things first, study is your priority. It's OK to work as long as you balance it with your assignments and revision. Remember how many hours of study you are meant to put in for each module, sometimes up to 15 hours. If you are doing four modules you can see how it all adds up. Thinking like this will help you to work out a realistic amount of time you have to do a job alongside your other commitments. I worked a lot through university at more than one job and I don't recommend doing that at all – one is enough! Even though I was able to provide for myself, I was tired out more than the average student and I didn't have much time to spend with my friends.

If you are going to work part time while you study, weekends are a good choice. You can always work full time in the holidays. If you work at weekends then you can concentrate on university work and extracurricular activities during the week. As your timetable becomes less crowded in your final year it can be tempting to increase your workload, but this is the wrong thing to do – really you should be doing the opposite and decreasing your hours at work.

Sometimes you really do have to make a sacrifice for your studies and put that new games console or pair of boots on hold. You'll find that you have to choose between extra hours at work and extra hours of study. It will be difficult, but try to focus on what you are truly investing in.

It's all about keeping the work/study balance healthy. If you do paid work in the day, set aside time in the evening for university work, and vice versa. Something I learnt

> (⁙) **Inside tip**
>
> **'Don't turn your nose up at working in a fast-food restaurant or corner shop. Every little helps and they'll probably be more able to work your shifts around university than a retail store.'**
>
> *Zaqoub, 20, Birmingham*

> (⁙) **Inside tip**
>
> **'Just because your friends work loads it doesn't mean you should too. Each degree subject is different and requires different amounts of study and application – do what works best for you!'**
>
> *Jake, 22, London*

was that just because you only have a few hours contact time, like four or five hours of lectures a week, that doesn't mean that the rest of the time is free. Remember, you have your assignments and eventually a dissertation to get on with.

I know many a student who could have got a first if they'd spent more time getting their head into study mode. The students I advise always ask me how to get a first and I always say it takes *time*. If you put in the time and make use of all the extra facilities available to you at university and beyond, you can achieve a first.

If you don't get into that mindset it will become so easy to say 'I'll do it later' or 'I still have a week to go'. But when you're working as well as studying, that week turns into a matter of hours and you never have a full day free. So be wise with your time.

Working at your university

Working at your university makes sense – after all, you do spend quite a bit of time there already. Every university has a job section on its website and you might be able to sign up to email alerts that let you know when a job becomes available. Alternatively, you may see a poster every once and a while offering hours to students. Look out for these, as they are great opportunities and the pay isn't too bad – especially if the job is in the administration or support section of the university.

> 📖 **The inside story: 'Hi, can I help you?'**
>
> I worked in my university library. It was well-paid work and I enjoyed it. Although it wasn't many hours, I did get to know loads about the library and it did make my study life a lot easier. I could find books quickly, make reservations and even use the photocopier without jamming it like I did before.

Here are my suggested top ten jobs at university:

1 Library assistant – good money, but quite strenuous work. May have to work unsocial hours and late nights.

2 Student ambassador – looks great on your CV.

3 University representative – instant CV builder and confidence booster.

4 Freshers' bar staff – handy because the hours will fit around your studies and you get to meet loads of new people. Plus you can take your bar experience abroad if you go travelling – bar staff are pretty much always needed.

5 Teaching assistant – these are extremely rare jobs so if you can get one go for it. It's a great opportunity to start on the teaching ladder and the position of responsibility looks great to future employers.

6 Helpline operator – more students than you think use the university helpline or nightline. It's great that this facility exists, but it wouldn't if it didn't have trained staff to handle to the calls.

 Career builder

Could you keep your university job when you graduate? Could you take your experience to another university?

💬 **Inside tip**

'When you start a new job, let them know whether or not you can work in the holidays. That way your employer knows in advance and can fit you in more easily when more hours come along and you have the time to do them.'

Ceylon, 20, Bury

7 Events staff – every university holds events like meetings, talks and shows. Staff are needed to help at these events and who better than a student who can represent the university and not get lost when showing people around?

8 Shop assistant – most campuses have a shop on campus and you could work there.

9 Gym assistant – good membership perks and keep fit at the same time.
10 Proofreader – this is actually a good little earner if you're an English student. You'll probably have noticed posters around campus with tear-off strips? In your second year you might want to put something like this up. You can learn to be more critical with your own assignments and generate some pocket money at the same time.

Working outside university

A lot of my friends worked in bars while they were at university – the hours suited them and they could work really flexible shifts. Some of them worked in shops and restaurant work was also very popular.

Whatever you do, make sure that you're happy. I've been in a job I didn't like and it's no fun – no matter how much you're getting paid. If there's a problem that you can't resolve with your boss, think carefully before you stay. Being miserable will affect your academic and social life, and you don't want anything to jeopardise that. If you ever do feel down about work or university life, make sure that you speak with a counsellor or a chaplain; they are trained to help.

> 💬 **Inside tip**
>
> 'Before you do any job "on the side", check with HMRC to find out if you need to register as self-employed.'
>
> *Ekaterina, 24, London*

Working in a shopping centre close to your campus or halls is a good idea, because a lot of the staff will be students and it may be easier to swap and change shifts if your employer is used to employing students. Also, the centre is local so there's less travelling and that gives you more time to use for other activities.

Becoming an au pair and babysitting can also work around your schedule. Websites like www.gumtree.com often have advertisements for nannies. Always check that everything is legal and above board before you work outside the PAYE (Pay

As You Earn) system. I worked as a tutor and had to register myself as self-employed alongside my PAYE-taxed job. Do your research before committing to anything.

Tutoring

Although you may not have graduated, remember that you still have a wealth of experience. You might be able to tutor someone who needs help preparing for their GCSEs, AS or A-levels. Even if you feel that your qualification is basic, there will always be someone who needs help with their studies. You will be passing on your skills and enhancing someone else's learning.

> 💬 **Inside tip**
>
> 'In my third year I really needed a job that fitted around my dissertation, so I decided to give tutoring a try. I put up a leaflet in the local coffee shops to advertise my skills and soon I got a few calls. I worked out the right time and pay and I've never looked back.'
>
> *Kev, 22, York*

Depending on your experience and skill, you could get a pretty decent wage doing this. If you feel unsure about private individual tutoring, how about joining a Saturday school or tutoring company to learn the ropes and see if it's what you want to do? Have a look online for Saturday school or tutoring companies like Kumon in order to get started.

Your CV

If the thought of creating a curriculum vitae or CV is daunting, check out the information on www.direct.gov.uk or consult an employability adviser at your university. If that doesn't help, my friend and the author of *7 Keys to a Winning CV: How to Create a CV That Gets Results*, Mildred Talabi, says that 'writing a winning CV is a skill that can be learnt'. Here are her seven great keys for producing an amazing CV:

Key no. 1: Know your target

Generic CVs don't work. Your whole CV should be geared towards the industry you would like to work in and the type of job you would like to have within this. The previous experience and skills you emphasise should be tailored to your target.

Key no. 2: Get in order

Your information should be arranged in a way that is clear, structured and tailored to your industry. A skills-based CV layout where your skills are the main focus works best for most sectors.

Key no. 3: Engage people in your introduction

Your introduction should be a very quick summary of who you are, what you've done and what the employer can hope to see in the rest of your CV. Think of it like a trailer to a movie or a blurb on the back of a book – keep it short, sweet and to the point, with no more than two or three sentences.

Key no. 4: Reveal your skill

A skill is something you are good at, whether naturally or developed by training. When listing your skills, it is very important to remember that a skill does not have to come from a work environment – often extra-curricular activities such as community or voluntary work or religious membership give you vital transferable skills that you can include on your CV.

Key no. 5: Looks can kill

Content is king, but presentation is also very important. The key is to make your CV as clear and as easy to read as possible. When choosing fonts, avoid Times New Roman as it is very outdated. Go for more modern fonts such as Tahoma and Verdana; Arial only if you really have to.

Key no. 6: Check it out

Mistakes in spelling and grammar are a big turn-off for employers, so be diligent about getting everything right. Don't rely too much on the Microsoft Word spelling and grammar checker, as this can sometimes be inaccurate. If in doubt, get a fresh pair of eyes to look over your CV.

Key no. 7: Sell, don't suffocate

There is no need to include absolutely everything you've ever done on your CV, only what is relevant to your target market (remember key number one). Two pages is the best length for a CV; three if you really need the extra space. The few exceptions include academic and technical CVs, which can, and often need to be, much longer.

Writing up a CV isn't as hard as it used to be. Creating covering letters and filling out application forms are all part of the job search process. Always make sure that you read the job brief and try not to cut, copy and paste a standard cover letter. You could be missing out on promoting yourself properly if you don't keep what you say fresh. In addition, if you're filling out an application form read and reread the guidance notes provided to ensure that you don't miss anything. Check and recheck your finished application – there's nothing worse than an employer talking a shine to your CV and then finding that the contact number is missing the last digit.

Getting the job you need

Sometimes you will have to take a job that's convenient – the job you need rather than the job you want. Stacking shelves in Tesco may not be the job you want, but if it is local it may mean that you can spend more time on your university work. While you're studying, the less taxing the job, the better. Complicated jobs lead to more hours thinking about the job than actually working there, and you don't want that. Choose something light that you can find enjoyment in. Even if it's working from home, find something you can stick at.

For job-finding websites and further advice, check out the useful resources at the back of this book. Remember that as tempting as it may be to work extra hours, that is time you could be putting towards your degree – which is by far your biggest investment to date. Put that first.

8

Mind and Body

This chapter is devoted to *you*. Your student life will be full of new experiences and situations that could unbalance your health: emotionally, physically, spiritually and mentally. When you're feeling down, come back and have another read of the chapter to refresh yourself.

When you're at university staying healthy may not be at the top of your priority list. The word 'health' applies to much more than what's going on inside your body. The stress created by exams, assignments, deadlines and revision can affect your health, and moving away from home and starting new relationships can cause extra stress. Fortunately, there are lots of good ways to stay on top of it all. If things get too much, don't hide it or try to deal with it alone, share your problems with someone and get help.

Mind

Mental health

The stress and tension of university life can get to you and leave you feeling a little disorientated. University gives you time to really think about your purpose in life and what you are going to do with your future. The stress of relationships, work and deadlines while all this is going on can be overwhelming.

If you are feeling continually worried or depressed, speak to a counsellor at your university or visit www.mind.org.uk. Mind is an organisation that 'helps people take control of their mental health'. Its website is really informative and there is an email address – info@mind.org.uk – and an information line that you can call on 0300 123 3393.

I've felt worried and stressed and had thoughts going round and round in my head, and this caused me many sleepless nights as well as a lack of concentration. When I spoke to someone else about what was going on and they listened, without judging me, it really helped. I definitely advise it. Seeking help doesn't mean that you're weak or weird, it means that you are taking control and are pursuing a healthy mindset – and there's nothing wrong with that!

> 💬 **Inside tip**
>
> 'I used to make things bigger than they needed to be and it used to get me down. I learnt to let the small things that I can't change go and look forward instead of back. I'm in my last year of university now and doing this has really helped me stay positive and on top of things.'
>
> *Baz, 21, Lincoln*

> ⓘ **Need to know...**
>
> *Coping with Stress at University: A Survival Guide* (2006), by Stephen Palmer and Angela Puri, published by Sage, is an excellent book. Written in a friendly, non-patronising way, it's a book that really helps you navigate through stressful times and learn how to avoid all the hassle next time.

Stress

It's easy to get stressed, especially around exam times or when your assignments are due. Stress can actually help you to become more organised, because you want to avoid the pressure!

Here are my top seven stress busters:

- ☯ Get laughing – put on a DVD of your favourite comedian or series and enjoy yourself.
- ☯ Refresh yourself with water and a walk. This clears your head and hydrates your brain.
- ☯ Talk with a friend about how their day was instead of thinking about the situation that's stressing you out.

> 🙂 **Inside tip**
>
> **'It may seem weird, but stress actually helps me get my work done quickly and I seem to do better when I'm under pressure.'**
>
> *Mikey, 20, Leeds*

- ☯ Make use of all the bath stuff you got last Christmas – run a bath, grab your iPod and make a 'do not disturb' sign. Enjoy your 'me' time.
- ☯ Get yourself looking your best and get some friends round or go out with them.
- ☯ Put some tunes on and sing along while you tidy your room – clearer room, clearer mind.
- ☯ Write in your journal or watch a video of your role model or the person you aspire to be like.

Body

Exercise

Most universities have a gym on campus that you can visit, and membership fees will be pretty low.

If you're going to start an exercise routine, speak to the staff at the gym or your GP and see if they have any advice for you to help things run smoothly. Your GP can give you a full check-up, which may include finding out your BMI (Body Mass Index).

Using a chart you can find out whether your BMI is too high or too low for your height and weight, and if necessary do something about it. Exercise and a good diet go hand in hand and they work best if they're balanced.

But you don't have to go to the gym to exercise and staying fit doesn't have to be boring. Dancing for a few hours in a club burns a lot of calories. Do a dance workout with your friends or get everyone over to use an exercise program on a games console. It's fun and you work out at the same time.

> 💬 **Inside tip**
>
> 'Even if I went for a short jog around the park or up and down my road, I ended up feeling so much better than if I hadn't. Also, you don't need expensive branded clothes — as long as you wear supportive running trainers, bright colours or stuff with reflective bits on, you're good to go.'
>
> *Phil, 21, Brighton*

> ☺ **Pocket money generator**
>
> Can you put your dance or fitness skills to use? If you study dance or enjoy exercising to music, how about starting a cheap fun exercise class for fellow students? Hire out a space, charge £2 on the door, everyone has fun and you create a weekly income. Remember to do warm-up and warm-down stretches!

Smoking

Smoking is known to cause heart disease and lung cancer and even to lower your sperm count if you're male, plus it's damaging to your pocket.

It can be tempting to reach for the cigarettes when university stress is getting on top of you, but instead try to talk to your friends or family about how you feel. Keep mints or a healthy snack on you to munch when you get a craving. Also there are loads of alternatives to help you quit. Nicotine gum and patches are two of the most popular options to try. If you want help quitting, log onto the NHS website at www.nhs.uk and search for 'smoke free'.

Alcohol

Alcohol is difficult to avoid at university. It's everywhere – in the fridge in your kitchen, at the bar, at parties, even at some award shows and special talks. It's easy to get carried away, literally, at parties, but before you go out think about how much you are going to drink. If you have a limit in mind, it may make it easier for you to keep track of how much you are drinking.

Here are some guidelines for staying safe:

- If you are in a nightclub or at a house party, in fact anywhere there are loads of people plus alcohol, make sure that you keep an eye and a hand on your drink. Some real lowlifes could spike your drink and this could be really harmful to your health.
- Try not to mix your drinks.
- Don't mix drink and drugs – even mixing alcohol with prescription drugs can have a negative effect, so always check the label on your medication or ask your doctor first.
- Keep hydrated by drinking water throughout the night. I try to drink one alcoholic drink then water and so on and have never had a hangover.
- Line your stomach with a good meal before you go out – a cup of milk can also do the job if you're in a hurry.
- Stay with your friends, don't go off on your own.
- Always have your mobile phone charged and your keys tucked away safely.
- I know it's probably been drummed it into you by now, but don't go anywhere with a stranger, whatever they are offering. If you have to go anywhere, let your friends know where you are going.

> ☺ **Inside tip**
>
> 'Getting merry before you go out is fun, but don't go overboard on the booze otherwise you'll end up staying in!'
>
> *Robbo, 19, London*

The NHS advises that men should not regularly drink more than three to four units a day and women should not regularly drink more than two to three units a day. Get its alcohol tracking app for the iPhone by clicking on www.nhs.uk/Tools/Pages/iphonedrinks.aspx. The tool is also available as a desktop application at www.nhs.uk/Tools/Pages/NHSAlcoholtracker.aspx.

If you are out drinking and you feel strange, like your drink has been spiked, tell your friends and the person behind the bar. It may prevent others being spiked. Adding any drug to a drink is illegal and subject to a penalty of up to 10 years in prison, not to mention the effects on the person who has been spiked.

If your drink has been spiked, get to a safe place, preferably home, with the help of your friends or a trusted person. Depending on which drug your drink has been spiked with, you may feel drowsy and disorientated, so do not go anywhere alone. If you are on your own, ask the bar staff for help to call a close friend or an ambulance, depending on how you feel. Report the incident to the police as soon as possible, because they can take samples of your blood and urine to find out what drug has been used.

ⓘ Need to know...

Many lives are lost each year because of people who drink and drive. Don't risk it yourself and don't ever get in a car with someone who has been drinking and then tries to get behind the wheel. Even if you think you are OK, you won't know that until your judgement is tested, and why risk it? Just don't drink and drive. Visit www.drinkaware.co.uk for more information and guidance on the dangers you can avoid by drinking responsibly.

💬 Inside tip

'When I go out clubbing I never leave my drink unattended and if I'm drinking from a bottle I use my thumb to cover the top. I don't accept drinks from people I don't know. As I'm usually out with quite a crowd, we all keep an eye on each other.'

Flo, 22, London

Drugs

I've seen at first hand how illegal drugs affect people, and it can be devastating for both the user and everyone around them. From what I've seen, drugs like cannabis are often the starting point towards Class A drugs like heroin and cocaine. Even if you have experimented with drugs in the past, see university as a fresh start. The bottom line is that drugs are illegal. They can also lead to death – so stay well away.

I had a friend who pretty much lived off ProPlus and coffee when assignments deadlines came about, but prescription and over-the-counter preparations like ProPlus can be dangerous too if used to excess, as well as the many cheap energy drinks that are available. These drinks give you a momentary buzz, but in the long term they aren't good for your body or mind.

Eating disorders

> 📖 **The inside story: My stress diet**
>
> To let you know how easy it is to slip into an eating disorder, I'm going to share my story. My intake was way below even the amount of calories needed for a healthy lifestyle and it could have led to an illness like anorexia if I hadn't put a stop to it when I did.
>
> I was in a situation where I was under a lot of pressure, so I decided to sort out my weight (I wasn't overweight at all). I was extremely stressed and I just 'forgot to eat' or didn't eat enough on purpose.
>
> In my mind I needed to 'sort something out', but in reality I was making up for my lack of control over the situation I was in and instead trying to gain that notion of control by focusing on my weight. Before I knew it I was consuming just a double espresso, a cup of soup and half a panini a day, then running pretty much every night. I lost two stone very quickly.
>
> When I look at photos now I can see that I was too thin, and I know that I was under too much pressure.
>
> It doesn't matter whether you are male or female, eating in a disordered way can affect anyone. And it can creep up on you. I got

out of it by telling someone I trusted and was close to what was going on. As soon as it was out I felt better about myself. I didn't need to control what I ate so severely and I gradually got back to eating in a way that was good for me. I started to change the situation I was in rather than letting it control me.

If you are doing any of the following, speak to someone about it, because you could have an eating disorder, or the beginnings of one:

- Eating then vomiting up your food on purpose because you think it will stop weight gain.
- Severely controlling what you are eating and not eating even when you feel extremely hungry.
- Binging/pigging out on sweet, sugary food, then vomiting it up or hiding the evidence of binges on a regular basis.
- Thinking about food and its effects for most of your day.

Speak to a trusted friend and then your doctor about what's going on and get some help and advice.

Sunbeds

Using a sunbed can be harmful to your skin in the long run and the leathery look at 24 is not attractive. I had a friend who was addicted to sunbeds, going on them three times a week. As well as it eating into her cash, she ended up having to have a few of her moles checked out because they had changed in size and colour.

> 💬 **Inside tip**
> 'Don't forget to stay in touch with your old friends when you go to university. They know you more than the people you've just met. Speak to them when you're down and visit them often.'
> *Chantelle, 26, Roehampton*

> 💬 **Inside tip**
> 'If you have a bad experience in a club, give it a miss next time and try somewhere new you've never been to before – you may prefer it!'
> *Zara, 19, Leeds*

Embrace your natural skin tone and use the spare cash to treat yourself to a cocktail when you're out instead.

If you're not quite ready to live in the skin you're in, you can always fake it. Fake tan, when applied correctly, can give you a healthy glow. If you're cautious, go for a tinted moisturiser and then build up to a gradual self-tanning lotion.

Partying

Partying and clubbing are a normal part of student life. They're a great way to let off steam, display your dance moves and get out and about. Check out the section on alcohol earlier in this chapter for ways to stay safe while out clubbing.

If you're going to throw a house party, make sure that *all* housemates are in agreement about the party happening. It's difficult to gauge the success of a house party because you never know who's going to show up. Naturally, if the police show up you know things aren't going in the direction of 'house party legend' status.

Make sure that you're all in agreement about the clean-up as well as the party! Here a few tried-and-tested tips for the party and the aftermath:

- Don't leave your stuff out on display – this includes laptops, phones, medication, cameras and so on. All that kind of stuff should be locked away somewhere safe, because once it's gone it's very difficult to get it back.
- Take photos so you can have memories of your party.
- Try to keep food and drink in the kitchen, as this is probably the most wipable place.
- Have as many bins as possible around the house – or at least one upstairs and one downstairs.
- Have a mop and cloths ready for spillages.

There are cheaper alternative to clubbing and partying. Try out a comedy night or open mic night with your friends. Or how about a games night? You'll be surprised how competitive people can be! Get the Monopoly, Wii or games consoles out, add snacks and let the fun begin.

For another cheap night in, get everyone to bring snacks to share, set up a projector or a big screen, open some bottles of wine and put a movie on. Movie night film suggestions include:

- Anything directed by Quentin Tarantino
- *Ferris Bueller's Day Off* – a classic 1980s film
- *The Breakfast Club* – another classic
- *Taken* or the Bourne trilogy – good action
- *The Fly*
- *Catch Me if You Can* (Leonardo DiCaprio)
- Guy Ritchie's Sherlock Holmes films – clever and really good camera work
- *Shaun of the Dead* and *Hot Fuzz* – great for letting off steam and laughing together
- *Rumble in the Bronx* – Jackie Chan classic
- *Howl's Moving Castle* or *Spirited Away* – Studio Ghibli anime movies

> ⌂ **Inside tip**
> 'If you're having a house party, make sure you put up signs to where the loos are to avoid any "accidents".'
>
> *Rachael, 21, Belfast*

> ⌂ **Inside tip**
> 'At Uni we were skint most of the time. When we wanted to all get together we would bring over a few Twister games and some wine – we always ended up having a proper laugh.'
>
> *Emma, 19, Manchester*

Relationships and sex

Relationships

University life is full of relationships of various types, so don't be afraid to get to know all different people.

Being friends is always a good place to start a dating relationship. Getting to know someone is easier when you are in their class or study at their campus. And going out together doesn't have to be expensive:

- Save splashing out for big victories. Instead, look out for two-for-one deals and voucher websites.
- Watch a rented movie with homemade popcorn and a duvet instead of going to the cinema.
- If your mate or date has a deadline coming up, how about leaving an encouraging note or favourite snack in their room to keep them going?

Sex

Sex is normal and natural, but there are a few things to remember to keep it worry free:

- Always use contraception – all sex should be safe sex. Carry your own in case the other person doesn't have any.
- Remember that just because it may seem like everyone is having sex, you don't have to. You don't have to do anything until you are ready. It's easy to think that because you are at university you have to experiment with everything and everyone, but that simply isn't true.
- Respect yourself and other people. Remember that sex is emotional as well as physical.

There is a lot of free contraception available. Condoms, the coil and the contraceptive pill are just a few of the most common types of contraception. If you are female, even if you are on the pill or have a coil fitted, always use a condom to avoid sexually transmitted diseases. Since everyone is different, what works for one person may not work for you too. The best thing to do is to go down to your local sexual health or GUM (Genito-Urinary Medicine) clinic and have a chat with the doctor or nurse, who will be happy to help.

> (⋯) **Inside tip**
> **'Always use contraception!'**
> *Nikki, 23, Salford*

It's good to talk with trusted friends about your sexual health, but they can't offer the same advice as a trained doctor or nurse, who may be able to spot something they can't.

The morning-after pill

The morning-after pill is emergency contraception and should not be taken on a regular basis. You can take it up to 72 hours after unprotected sex, but the sooner you take it the more effective it will be.

Smear tests

However embarrassed or uncomfortable you feel about doing so, it is important for all women to have cervical screening or a smear test, as it's more widely known. The test is used to detect abnormal cells in your cervix. The nurse will make you feel comfortable and will talk you through what will happen. Most tests will have routine and normal results, but you won't know until you go.

According to the NHS, 'In the UK, cervical cancer is the second most common cancer in women under 35 (after breast cancer). About 2,800 women a year are diagnosed with cervical cancer.' This isn't something to be taken lightly and this is a test you should definitely make time for. If you are nervous, ask your friends about it, or do some research and then make an appointment.

> (i) **Need to know...**
>
> To find out more about cervical cancer and getting tested, check out www.jostrust.org.uk. It's a really good website that has loads of information about cervical screening and pap/smear tests. The site even explains what the cervix is.

Testicular cancer and breast cancer

Lads, get to know your balls. Testicular cancer can be detected by checking your testicles on a regular basis. According to the Channel Four programme *Embarrassing Bodies*, those aged between 18 and 35 are most at risk. Check out www.channel4embarrassingillnesses.com for a guide to checking and the signs and symptoms. Start by feeling for abnormal hard lumps, bumps or changes in your private area. If you find anything strange, don't ignore it, stay calm and pay a visit to your doctor.

Ladies, get to know your breasts. Checking for abnormalities should be part of your shower routine. You can also go to www.channel4embarrassingillnesses.com for more information. If you detect a lump or unusual swellings, don't ignore them, ring your doctor for an appointment to check them out.

Sexually transmitted infections

Sexually transmitted infections (STIs), also called sexually transmitted diseases (STDs), are one of the most common consequences of having unprotected sex. Remember that not all infections are transmitted through sex – for example, sharing a razor with someone who has been infected can lead to you getting the infection too. There are many types of infections, described below.

HIV and AIDS

HIV stands for human immunodeficiency virus, a virus that basically destroys the immune system. It prevents your body from fighting infections and diseases. It is spread through sexual contact – not just vaginal, but oral and anal too.

AIDS stands for acquired immune deficiency syndrome and occurs at a late stage of the HIV virus, when the immune system has stopped working. It can lead to serious complications and even death.

Syphilis

Syphilis is passed on through contact with an open syphilis sore. These sores are located around the genitals and even the lips and mouth. Sometimes the sores don't appear immediately once someone is infected, so if you are sexually active regular sexual health checks are a must. If you see anything that looks suspicious on a sexual partner, ask before you do anything else!

Hepatitis B and C

Hepatitis is another infection spread through sexual contact and bodily fluids. There is an extra high risk for needle sharers. It affects the liver and is often caused by a virus. Hepatitis B can be treated and even vaccinated against; Hepatitis C is more serious and can lead to long-term liver damage.

Chlamydia

Chlamydia is one of the most common sexually transmitted infections, once again passed on through unprotected sex. The symptoms of chlamydia are sneaky. You may not be able to tell that you have the infection, or whether a partner has, which is why it is so important to have regular checks and always to use a condom.

> **ⓘ Need to know...**
>
> Chlamydia is most common in young people – under 25s, to be exact. So a large majority of students fit into this age bracket. The good news is that if you are under 25 you can get tested for chlamydia for free, and the test is completely confidential. You can even get a testing kit by post.
>
> To find out more visit www. chlamydiascreening.nhs.uk. The site even has a snazzy 'hide' button if you don't want anyone else to see what you're reading.

Genital herpes

The symptoms of genital herpes are not always visible and the infection can remain dormant for months or even years, another reason for using a condom whenever you have sex. The infection sometimes manifests itself as blisters or an outbreak of sores on your private area or even around your mouth. If you have any of these symptoms, visit your sexual health clinic straight away.

> **📖 The inside story: Harry**
>
> 'To be fair I had slept with quite a few girls in my first year but never had any kind of symptoms, so I didn't worry about how many people I slept with – how stupid was I?
>
> After I heard some rumours about a girl I had been with a few weeks ago and some strange bumps appeared around my pubic area, I went to the GUM clinic. Before I went I searched for the bumps online just to get an idea of what it might be. But there were so many things it looked like, I decided just to go and speak to the nurse.

I felt a bit embarrassed in the waiting room, but I'd rather know than keep on worrying about it and that's why I had the balls to go (pun intended).

The nurse examined me and said that the bumps were a symptom of genital warts. I was gutted: because the area around the condom had made contact with the carrier, I still got the virus. And I didn't know if it was the girl I'd just slept with or someone else before that, as the warts don't always come up immediately.

After that I always had to tell the person I was going to sleep with that I had genital warts. At times I was really depressed, because I felt so down about it and felt like I was on my own with the virus. Some of my friends didn't tell girls they were sleeping with about infections they'd had, but it just felt wrong to keep that from someone you wanted to be with. Each girl has reacted differently, and sometimes it's uncomfortable, but it's better than seeing someone else have to go through what I've been through.'

To find out more information about any of these sexual infections (plus more information on any symptoms you may have that aren't mentioned here), book an appointment with your local sexual health clinic, speak to a close friend or do some research on the NHS website. Whatever you do, don't ignore the problem and don't feel embarrassed. Type in www. nhs.uk/Livewell/studenthealth for pages specifically designed for you.

Sleep

It's commonly said that the average human needs eight hours of sleep a night. I don't know about you, but as a student I hardly ever got a full eight hours! Whether it was a fire alarm, party or cramming, there was usually something to keep me awake.

Here are my top tips for getting a good night's sleep:

- ☙ Invest in a pair of earplugs or headphones.
- ☙ Drink some herbal tea, such as camomile or blackcurrant.

- ⮑ Turn off all your electronic gadgets, like your laptop and so on.
- ⮑ Set the alarm on your clock or phone so that you don't have to worry about oversleeping.
- ⮑ Try and get your outfit for the next day ready the night before – I *know* how difficult this can be, but trying is good.
- ⮑ Try not to eat too late – remember that your body has to work to digest that late-night pizza, not leaving it much time to rest and repair.
- ⮑ Don't worry – I remember someone saying that 'worry is like a rocking chair, it gives you something to do but gets you nowhere.'

> **💬 Inside tip**
>
> 'I drink a big glass of water before I go to bed and the same again in the morning, but I add a slice of lemon. It works especially well for me after a late night because it makes me feel really refreshed.'
>
> *Lana, 20, Durham*

> **👤 Career point**
>
> Can you use your experiences to help someone else? How about working for your university nightline? You can help others, develop listening skills, and perhaps start a career in counselling.

Soul

Your personal well-being is very important and how you feel within yourself can get unsettled at university. It's a new place away from all you know for the next three years. University will change your outlook on life and possibly shape your future into something you never thought it could be.

Here are ten keys to keeping in touch with yourself while at university:

- ⮑ Write down a plan of what you want to be and where you want to be ultimately – no matter how wishful or extravagant. When you feel out of sorts, take the plan out and have a look to remind yourself of where you're heading.
- ⮑ Keep photos of your friends, family and special people around your room to remind you that they are on your journey along with you.

- ☝ If you have a faith, try not to lose it at university. If you visit a place of worship regularly at home, try to carry on in your new town or city. There may even be a club, union or society you can join so you can grow and add to your faith.
- ☝ Take care of yourself – stick your headphones in and go for a run, start cycling on sunny days.
- ☝ Take time out. If you need to spend time with your family over the summer rather than going on holiday with your friends, do it. Do what's best for you.
- ☝ Be authentic – sooner or later people will know if you are faking it.
- ☝ Self-esteem and self-belief come from you, not other people.
- ☝ The past is the past, so leave it there and don't let it control your future.
- ☝ If you're feeling down, put on a comedy DVD (*The Office* always brings me out of my woes) and laugh out loud.
- ☝ Volunteering is a good way to learn new things, meet new people and generally help others. I volunteered for Oxfam for two years and as well as finding lots of vintage goodies, I knew I was helping people who had a more difficult life than me. It helped me keep things in perspective.

Looking after yourself at university is a challenge, especially when you're away from friends and family and catapulted into a new world. Remember that deep down inside, everyone is in the same boat, even though some may not show it.

If you choose to see university life that way it will be easier to feel balanced. When you feel the scales tipping to one side or the other, speak with someone you trust and let them know what's bothering you – they may be able to help. Never go it alone, because you'll find yourself going round in circles.

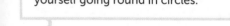
to *Student* to *Student* to *Student*

9

Changes

Each student's journey through university life is different. Everyone comes from a different background and has different dreams and aspirations. In this chapter I hope to bring to light some of the changes you may face and offer help with improving situations that may seem challenging.

The environment at university shapes you and changes you and as a person you will grow and develop. My degree changed the way I looked at myself and what I thought I could achieve. I really enjoyed my course and my lecturers were so helpful. They also recognised a talent in me that I'd always thought I couldn't use. When I started getting excellent grades in my creative writing, I remembered the books I'd written as a child and the poems I'd crafted. I decided to go with what I loved and that's what led me to change my degree, choose creative writing as my major and move universities. My friend Lucy made a similar decision and she agreed to share her story.

📖 The inside story: **Lucy**

In 2009, I started my BA Hons degree in Journalism and Creative Writing. After studying media at college, I chose to study journalism because it was something that came naturally to me. However, after several months I accepted that the course was not for me; I was very unhappy with the creative writing units and was not enjoying university life at all. I decided to try to change my course, and consulted one of the university advisers about switching to Film, TV and Radio Studies (FTVRS), a course that appealed to me as it was fairly practical.

I was unable to change my course with immediate effect because I had already missed half of the first year. I had assumed I would be able just to transfer to my new course and literally start going to lectures and seminars straight away, as it was April and the start of a new semester. However, I was left with a difficult decision to make; either intermit until September, which is basically dropping out until the next academic year; or finish my first year of Journalism and Creative Writing in order for me to go into year two of my new course.

I decided I was not going to continue with my course, I would rather drop out and return in September. September came round quickly and I started my new course. I was immediately disappointed. There were barely any practical units, I didn't make very many friends on my course, and there were lots of essays to do; much more than I had been assigned for Journalism and Creative Writing.

I felt I was stuck in a situation where I couldn't change my course again because the university wouldn't approve, but I didn't really want to drop out; nor did I want to continue on the course.

After some contemplation I just decided to go for it and complete my FTVRS course. I put my head down and finished my first year with good grades, even though I felt the course was not for me. I went home for the summer and was preparing for my second year when I received a letter from the Dean informing me that the university was getting involved in an issue with the landlord of the house we had moved out of. I spoke with the Dean's secretary and was informed that it was now a university matter.

I got very angry and thought to myself, 'I don't even like the university, I don't even want to go back, I want to do a new course.' So I contacted my local university and decided to do the course that I should have started in 2009: Screenwriting. I had always had a passion for it, and always written novels and scripts as a hobby, but I didn't see the point of studying it at university, because scriptwriting career opportunities are few and far between. But I decided that if I am going to attend university, I need to study something stimulating and interesting. I need to get a first-class degree in a subject I am passionate about, and I need to work hard to have a career doing what I love, regardless of how hard it might be to get my foot in the door. I sorted out a transfer to the local university, which was a lot easier than I expected, and I am currently approaching the start of year 2 in Film and TV Screenwriting there.

What I have learned from my university experience so far is that choosing the right course and the right university can be very hard, but it is never too late to make a change. Some people may complete their degree even though they are not entirely happy, but I decided that if I am going to pay so much for my education, then I need to do something worthwhile and enjoyable. Admittedly I can sometimes be a fickle person, but changing my course is the best thing I have done.

My best advice to someone who is not happy on their course is: talk to a student in year two or three of the course you are enrolled in to find out if the course gets better in year two, as many courses become more practical, or more focused on something you are interested in. I spoke to somebody in year two of FTVRS to find out if there were any good script writing units and they told me there weren't; this confirmed my decision to change course. Choosing a university and course is like choosing a product in a showroom. They will give you a guided tour of the buildings and show you all the facilities; they will make the course sound amazing in the prospectus and the course tutors will try and encourage you to choose their course. But the best overview of a particular university or course is one you will get from one of the students.

I know that's a long story, but I felt it was best to include every single bump in the road to encourage others who might be feeling the same. The point is that you're not alone. If you want to make your university life work for you, you will have to make some tough decisions.

Expectations

Sometimes your expectations of university just aren't met, and it's important to think about why this may be. Always try to look for a positive way to make changes. Failing exams doesn't mean the end of the world, for example, as there will most probably be a chance to do retakes. I know how disappointing it can be when you don't get the grade you want, but it gives you an opportunity to grow and learn when you know you haven't done your best.

If you do feel you have to make changes, the thing to remember is – don't rush. Sometimes emotions get in the way of sense and it's very easy to react instead of respond. I think as students we feel the pressure to fit in with everyone and just 'survive university', but really we should be enjoying our investment. We are putting a lot of our money and time into university, so it has to be right for us.

> 💬 **Inside tip**
>
> **'University helps you to mature and learn how to look after yourself – you have to constantly make decisions and choices that affect your life for ever.'**
>
> *Bibi, 22, Exeter*

What if things don't work out?

If something isn't right for you and is making you feel unhappy, definitely don't keep it to yourself. If it's the university or degree that's getting you down, speak to your course administrator and see what they can do to help; or, if you really want to leave, the careers adviser. It could be that you could change your modules or even change your major or minor subject.

If your housing isn't working out, speak to your landlord or university housing officer – they may be able to move you or deal with your complaint. It's normal not to get along with everyone, but if you're being bullied or people are targeting you and you have asked them to stop, it's best to move away from them. If it's a complaint that you have with the university, like a lecturer or the level of service you're receiving, definitely arrange to meet your tutor in their office hours and discuss what is bothering you.

If you aren't satisfied or you feel that things aren't moving forward positively, you can launch a formal complaint. This is normally a formal email or handwritten letter submitted to your head of department or head of school. If it is something that many people are experiencing, maybe speak with your friends and see what kind of action they are taking.

Sometimes the timing is just wrong. In my second year I made friends with a lovely girl on my course, we got along really well and shared a few common interests. She noticed a few things that she didn't feel were right for her on the course, and after a few weeks she had left. Was her decision wrong? No, not at all. If it's the whole course that isn't working for you, definitely consider your options and make changes. Some changes may be completely unstoppable – marriage, a death in your family or even relocation can force you to change your university.

> ### 💬 Inside tip
>
> **'I really enjoyed the changes that occurred through my time at university. Lecturers coming and going meant that we learnt new things from different people. Building work at the campus enabled us to have a new Learning Resource Centre and bus shelter. I think change at the university is good as well as change within yourself.'**
>
> *Cara, 29, London*

When you change your course or university, or when you leave university altogether, relationships with your friends will go through changes too. I went from a closeknit class of less than 10 to a class of over 500 and lectures with at least 100 students, none of whom I knew at first. Follow the advice in Chapter 2 about making friends and you'll soon start to fit in.

Many people give up too easily when they fail. I remember when I was in my third year, I failed my driving test twice – but I didn't give up. I took some time out to think about my options and finances and planned when to redo my test. Your degree can be seen in the same way: if you really need it and want it, you won't give up. If you do feel like giving up, perhaps speak to the chaplain or a counsellor at your university – maybe they can offer some advice on how to deal with the way you are feeling.

> 💬 **Inside tip**
>
> 'The chaplains aren't boring or out of touch, they listen to what you ask and take your questions and worries seriously.'
>
> *Sharon, 20, Leeds*

However you deal with your situation, try to stay positive about what you are going to do next. And don't panic or worry – changes prepare you for the choices you will have to make in the future.

> 💬 **Inside tip**
>
> 'When my girlfriend got pregnant at university we were both in our final year and really had to think about keeping the baby. After a lot of thought and advice from family, we decided we were going to take it all as it came as they would support us in our decision. Having a baby and juggling university work is hard, I can't imagine doing it alone. My tip is to speak to a counsellor at your university and your family to seek advice and help along the way – and try not to give up your studies if you can. You'll have more to offer the baby if you're a graduate and it's more difficult and expensive to go back and start a new degree in the future.'
>
> *Miguel, 23, Coventry*

Retaking a year

If you've failed a year, again don't panic, because you can always retake. You will also have a lot of experience under your belt, which will improve your chance of passing on your second try.

Book an office hour or two with one of your lecturers and discuss the next options. If you can't get hold of a lecturer or tutor, speak to the course administrator in your faculty office.

If you need to resit an exam, speak with your lecturer or tutor about when this may happen. It's best to know as soon as possible what the dates are so that you can revise and prepare.

Leaving your course

If you simply don't 'get' the course, perhaps have a serious think about if you want to continue. Take a few days to think about what you might do next. Speak with friends and family, but ultimately the decision must be yours.

It is difficult to make a decision like that and you may have doubts, but if you really feel that you need to do it, speak with a tutor or university adviser first, like Lucy did. Then leave the *right* way – calm and dignified, with a positive outlook towards your next course. Always notify your university in writing too.

If you really do want to leave your course, find out the following:

- ෮ Whether you can use any of the credits you've earnt so far towards the next course of your choice.
- ෮ How much you'll have to repay the university or Student Loan Company – if anything.
- ෮ Whether you need to fill out any forms. Normally you'll need a 'change of circumstances' form – you can find this at www.direct.gov.uk/studentfinance.

Remember, changes are part of growing up and definitely part of your university life – they can't be avoided! The way you deal with changes will affect the rest of your life too, so when things get a bit too much have another read of this chapter and see if there's anything that can help lighten the load.

The final chapter gives you a sneak peek into the world of graduates who have finished university and are hungry for work and success in the big bad world.

10

What Next?

ime really does go by quickly when you're at university, so it's good to look to the future. First of all, congratulations in advance! It will have been a long road and you will have changed so much since you started filling in your applications and waiting nervously for replies.

This last chapter collates all the graduate information I could lay my hands on. I've also covered my experience of graduating and what I did next to give you a taster of what may be ahead for you.

When you have finished your last assignment and sent it off, there will be such a feeling of satisfaction – but nervousness too. You're hoping you'll get the grades you want and worked for and if you do, what will you do next?

Whatever class of degree you get, don't let it overshadow the fact that you have just completed three years doing one of the highest recognised academic awards. You are a graduate – and it's an amazing feat. To show the determination to see something as intense as a degree through to the end is commendable.

Employers will recognise this determination. If you plan to be an entrepreneur, you can draw on your experience of seeing something through from beginning to end. If you want to start a family, you'll know that you can multitask. If you want to travel the world, you just might be able to earn a few extra bob teaching English!

Take a moment away from reading this to stop and think about what you have achieved so far. Be proud of yourself.

Inside tip

'I couldn't wait to finish university when I got to my final year – I was ready to move on and further my career. I was scared of what may come along, but my degree helped me feel more prepared.'

Talia, 20, Sussex

Graduation

Your graduation ceremony will be one of the proudest moments in your life. The gown and mortarboard don't come free, but they're worth it – you're only going to have this moment once in your life so you might as well invest in all the trimmings. Even if you're planning to do a postgraduate degree, you'll never be able to graduate from your first degree again.

Don't be shy of your achievement. Show up prepared, participate and be proud of yourself. Get papped – have your photos taken and show them off. It's a special day that's dedicated to your hard work, determination and academic success, so enjoy it with the people you care about the most.

The inside story: My graduation experience

I remember the booming 'Lauren Lucien' from across the stage, then everyone started clapping and I heard my husband giving a massive 'Woooo' from somewhere in the audience. Those few seconds were some of the proudest of my life. I'd been nervous waiting in line to walk across the stage (without tripping up) and shake the vice-chancellor's hand, but it was so worth it. I enjoyed every moment.

You may be the first in your family to receive a degree, and what you have, no one can take away from you. You are a graduate. If you didn't get the class of degree you were expecting or you had a rough final year, don't worry. You made it, you stuck at it and you saw it through until the end. You have lots of choice as a graduate. Celebrate with your friends, be positive and enjoy your new beginning.

> ⊙ **Inside tip**
> 'You will feel like a geek in your robes – but it's not embarrassing. I actually felt proud to be a geek!'
>
> *Marta, 22, Roehampton*

Where are you going?

Some students will have their life after university set out in a five-year plan, others just want a break from continuous study. If you're reading this part of the book in your first year, it may be an idea to start planning a few possible options for your graduate life. If you're reading this in your second or third year, it may be a good time to dig out that plan I mentioned in Chapter 8 under 'Soul' and see what you can add to it. Are you close to your original plan or has it changed entirely?

Your university should have a career adviser who can help you when it comes to the options available. But if you're not there yet, I'll set out a few possibilities in this chapter.

> ⌁ **Career builder**
> When you speak to your career adviser, ask if they can suggest any part-time jobs you can do within the university if you are going to stay on to do a Master's.

Postgraduate study

📖 **The inside story: My 'plan'**

I had the leaflets for my Master of Fine Arts (MFA) in Creative Writing in a specific folder on my desk – that was what I was going to do after my BA, no doubts. Well, maybe a tiny, tiny one that I kept shoving to the back of my mind. I applied anyway, to the university where I did my BA, and got an unconditional offer. I ticked that off my list and started looking at ideas for my future dissertation.

However, I didn't get the academic scholarship I had been relying on, which threw a spanner in the works. I wasn't successful at securing other sources of funding either. With no funding, I seriously had to consider whether this was what I really wanted to do. Now that I had to scrape together £10,000 from somewhere (I hadn't been successful at getting a career development loan), I had to make a new choice. In fact I started the course and then rapidly withdrew. The tiny, tiny doubt had become a very big doubt and I didn't want to waste time – or money.

You may ask, after all I've said in this book, 'You let a small thing like money defeat you?' I would be lying if I said that the fact it was half a deposit for a house didn't help me make up my mind a lot sooner. But the tiny, tiny doubt was: Is this what I really want to do and is this how I really want to go about it? In the end, I realised that I didn't want to do the MFA, and that I wanted to be a writer now and perhaps a teacher one day. I was already a writer and I already taught in some capacity, so I started looking for other options.

I ended up writing this book and then another. Now I'm looking forward to the next!

The availability of funding can sway your decision whether to go straight into postgraduate study. Many students end up taking a year out and earning, then returning to study able to pay for the full cost of their course.

If you do decide to work then continue studying, try to remember what you are working towards. When you start having more than enough money to live on, it's very tempting to stay where you are and not return to study.

If you just 'feel like you should' do a further degree, ask yourself whether it's what you really want. If you need to take some time out of education to think about it, then so be it. If you are an international student, maybe you need time back home; who knows, maybe there will be a better career path waiting for you there.

Master's degree

A Master's degree is the next step up from a bachelor's degree. There are several Master's degrees available, including MA (Master of Art), MSc (Master of Science) and MRes (Master of Research).

A standard Master's degree usually takes one to two years to complete, depending on whether you do a part-time or full-time course. Most Master's degrees have a taught element and a research element, resulting in the writing of a dissertation of around 15,000 words. An MRes has a greater research focus, with less teaching and a longer dissertation, usually of 35–40,000 words.

> (i) **Need to know...**
>
> If you want to have a look at possible Master's courses for you, check out www. findamasters.com. It's the biggest database I've found for Master's degrees and it's global. There's also www.findaphd. com, if you wanted to explore even further study. Both have information about courses and possible sources of funding.

PhD

After you complete a Master's degree you can pursue a PhD, the award of Doctor of Philosophy. Most universities require you to have at least a 2.1 in your undergraduate degree as well, but entrance requirements vary. In some subjects you can pursue a PhD with only a good undergraduate degree, so it's best to check with the university of your choice. PhDs come in all shapes and sizes, but the common factor is that they are achieved through research and the writing of a thesis, normally of between 80,000 and 100,000 words.

Teaching

Bear in mind that it is desirable to have grade A–C in Maths and also in English if you want to pursue a teaching career. If you don't, don't panic, you can always redo your GCSEs. I redid my Maths GCSE over a year at an adult education college and I actually enjoyed it the second time around.

Here are few ways into teaching just to get you started.

Postgraduate Certificate in Education

If you add a Postgraduate Certificate in Education (PGCE) to your BA or BSc, you are pretty much on the path towards being a teacher. Postgraduate teaching certificate courses are usually a year long; if you want you can do a Master's degree with the PGCE as part of your final qualification.

For a list of places where you can take a PGCE and what it entails, visit www.tda.gov.uk and type 'PGCE' into the search box.

> ### 😐 Inside tip
>
> 'I volunteered at the school nearest to my university in my second and third year. It was only one day a week, but I got experience that really helped me decide where to specialise as a teacher.'
>
> *Ben 20, London*

Graduate Training Programme

The Graduate Teaching Programme (GTP) allows you to gain Qualified Teacher Status while working in a paid teaching job – not to mention gathering vital training along the way. For more information on what the GTP is and where you can do it, type www.tda.gov.uk/get-into-teaching/teacher-training-options/gtp.aspx into your browser and have a look at what's on offer.

Teach First

The Teach First programme has the mission 'to address educational disadvantage by transforming exceptional graduates into effective, inspirational teachers and leaders in all fields'.

It is an excellent initiative that works in schools all over the UK. The charity, which operates in schools in the most challenging areas, offers graduates a two-year programme combining teaching and learning, leading to Qualified Teacher Status. For more information visit www.teachfirst.org.uk.

TEFL

TEFL stands for Teaching English as a Foreign Language and a TEFL certificate is a very popular qualification among graduates who want to live, study or travel abroad. You don't have to have a degree in English Language either! For more info on TEFL training and current vacancies, check out www.tefl.com.

Getting a job

Most students come out of their undergraduate degree with a sizeable amount of debt, and it's normal to want to start working straight away. However, it's not always easy to get a job and you have to consider all your options.

Internships

Some students are fortunate enough to have a internship lined up for when they graduate. I would suggest looking for these types of scholarships and internships early in your second year. Start planning and writing emails and letters to potential companies. Even if you feel like it's ridiculously early, it's best to get your application in as soon as possible.

Remember that internships are usually unpaid except for travelling expenses, so factor into your decision how you're going to support yourself while you're getting this kind of work experience. In some industries it's almost mandatory, though, and an internship can lead to a full-time job.

Volunteering

If you're feeling a bit tired of applying for jobs everywhere with no response, why not try volunteering? As well as Oxfam, I volunteered at the Barbican Children's Library while I was still doing my degree and used the experience to start working at my university library.

If there's a particular company you'd love to work at, perhaps volunteer to work there for free. I know that sounds daft, but it could work.

I remember an article on the news about a graduate who was sick of getting rejections, so he had put on his suit and paraded around the business district in London with a sandwich board, advertising himself for work. He did actually get offered a job. I'm not saying you should rob the nearest chippy of its menu board and make a DIY 'sell yourself' kit. Hopefully you will have built up some contacts while you're at university that you can call on to help you get a job. As long as it's legal, any idea is worth trying.

Graduate jobs

There are many websites that advertise jobs specifically for graduates. They also advertising graduate schemes and internships, so it's well worth taking a look to see what you might have the opportunity to do. Here are my top three:

- www.thebigchoice.com/ Graduate
- www.gradjobs.co.uk
- www.jobs.guardian.co.uk/ jobs/graduate/graduate- scheme

> 💬 **Inside tip**
>
> 'Working and volunteering through university kept my CV full and up to date. When I left I felt more confident about getting work than if I hadn't.'
>
> *Shola, 24, Brighton*

> 💬 **Inside tip**
>
> 'When you're coming towards the end of university it's normal to feel apprehensive – speak with a careers adviser and make a plan of what you may do when you've finished your course.'
>
> *Claire, 22, Loughborough*

Becoming an entrepreneur

We've all seen the television programme *Dragons' Den* – maybe you've got an idea for a business and would like to set up on your own?

My ten top tips for becoming an entrepreneur are these:

- Don't be afraid to dream – that's where all good business ideas start.
- It may be tempting to go maverick, but you need to be surrounded by a network of associates and friends and family.
- Get a good relationship going with your bank manager. Who knows what help you'll need in the future?
- Have a plan – write down what you want and when you want it, and how you are going to go about getting it.
- Learn from your mistakes and move on, taking your experience with you.
- Start with what you know. I knew about being at university, so I wrote a book about it. What do you know?
- Don't despise small beginnings, cherish them.
- Develop a passion for business.
- Learn how to handle both success and failure.
- Discover ways of motivating yourself, even when times are tough. Get out your book of big dreams or get away from your laptop and enjoy a coffee with a close friend.

> ### ⓘ Need to know...
> Searching for inspiration? Check out www.virgin.com/richard-branson/blog to enter the world of one of the world's most successful entrepreneurs, Richard Branson.

Travelling

After three years or more at university, at the top of your list may be broadening your horizons by going off to see the world. You may have saved money with this in mind, you may work through the summer after graduating to scrape some dosh together, or you may decide to look for work while you're travelling. Get all the information you need about working abroad at www.prospects.ac.uk/working_abroad.htm.

Here are my top ten tips for travelling:

🖰 Make sure you stay safe – be informed and be careful.

🖰 Don't go travelling alone. Go with a friend or a group of friends so you can all look out for each other.

🖰 Let people know where you are. Better yet, write a real-time blog on the move.

🖰 Take loads of photos to look back on and impress the kids!

🖰 Make sure that you have copies of your passport and official documents and keep the copies in a different place; better still, scan them and email the scans to yourself so you can access them electronically.

🖰 Travel with a secure bag that cannot be snatched easily and always zip it up.

🖰 If you have an amazing experience, why not offer to write a review – maybe you'll get an extra night at a hotel for it.

🖰 Pack only what you *need* – you don't want to be lugging around a heavy suitcase everywhere.

🖰 If you have a disability, enquire about access before you go to another country. Also look at the healthcare system and how it caters for people with disabilities.

🖰 Get travel insurance – I can't stress how important this is.

> 💬 **Inside tip**
>
> **'To me, taking a year out to travel with friends and having a proper break seems the best way to round off university life.'**
>
> *Will, 24, Cornwall*

> ⓘ **Need to know...**
>
> **If you are serious about travelling and have weighed up all the options, check out *The Backpacker's Bible*, revised edition (2008), by Suzanne King and Elaine Robertson, published by Anova.**

Final thoughts

Think about what you want out of your life and your career now that you have finished university. As entwined as these two aspects may become, never forget that what you do has to be what *you really want*. If you haven't finished your university life yet and you're just finishing this book as a first year – well, you're already ahead of the crowd.

University Dictionary

University has its own specialist language. Here's a mini-list of all the lingo I had to look up and learn – so you don't have to.

Academic adviser Part of a team that can help with your assignments and presentations.

Academic year The months between September and June.

Access to Learning Fund A fund that universities have to help students who are experiencing financial difficulties.

Alumni Graduates of the university.

Bachelor's degree An undergraduate-level degree, which has varying titles (such as BA and BSc) depending on the subject taken.

Book list The list of textbooks and materials you will need before you start each module.

Bursary An amount of money awarded to certain students by the university. It is based on financial need and it doesn't need to be paid back.

Campus Your university base. Sometimes a university will have multiple campuses.

Chaplain or chaplaincy The staff at the university who offer a religious support service.

Credits 'Points' that you get from your completed assignments, projects and dissertations.

Dean A head of department in the university.

Department A subject area within a faculty.

Dissertation Probably the longest piece of writing you'll do at university, normally in your final year as part of your degree.

Faculty A subject area or group of subjects. For example, the faculty of arts and social sciences may house journalism, creative writing, drama and so on.

First The highest degree grade that can be awarded.

Five second rule How long a food item can apparently remain on the floor before it can be picked up and eaten.

Graduate Someone who has graduated from university.

Graduation The ceremony at which you are awarded your degree.

Halls of residence Often abbreviated to 'halls', university accommodation where students stay in their first year.

Joint honours A degree in two subjects.

Lecture When students gather together in a lecture hall or classroom for a lesson.

LGBT Lesbian, gay, bi and transgender.

Major The main subject in a degree.

Master's degree A postgraduate-level degree, which has varying titles (such as MA or MSc) depending on the subject taken.

Means tested Financial help in proportion to your means or income.

Minor The secondary subject in the a honours degree.

Module A unit of a degree.

Mortar board A square hat with a big tassel that you wear with your graduation gown.

NUS National Union of Students.

Orientation The first part of term, designed to welcome new students.

PhD Doctor of Philosophy, a postgraduate-level degree that is awarded on the basis of research.

Plagiarism Unlawful reproduction of work that is not yours.

Postgraduate degree Further degree-level study taken after completing an undergraduate degree.

Professor A senior academic.

Reading week A week reserved for catching up on work, reading ahead and preparing for the next batch of assignments.

Self-plagiarism Reproduction of your own previously marked or used work in another assignment.

Semester An academic term, of which there are two or three a year.

Seminar A smaller lecture in which discussion is highly encouraged.

SU Abbreviation for Students' Union.

Term Another word for semester.

Thesis statement The part of an essay where the argument is made.

Transcript A printed record of all your marks and grades at university.

Tuition fees The total amount of money you have to pay for tuition at university.

Tutor A teacher who leads tutorials.

Tutorial A teaching session with a tutor and a small section of a class, more intimate than seminars or lectures.

Undergraduate degree A student's first degree.

Union Students' Union.

Vice-Chancellor The chief executive of the university.

Useful Resources

Accommodation and housing

www.accommodationforstudents.com A search engine for student accommodation, including private halls.

www.comparethemarket.com A comparison site for the best prices for insurance.

www.homesforstudents.co.uk Flat share, house share, and rooms to rent for students.

www.nationalcode.org Information on the code for student housing.

http://student.spareroom.co.uk A free student accommodation finder.

Bargains

www.amazon.co.uk Bargain books, DVDs and a whole lot more.

www.ebay.co.uk An online auction site for both buying and selling.

www.freecycle.org Free stuff to pick up and to swap.

www.groupon.co.uk Sign up for email alerts on special offers in your local area.

www.vouchercodes.co.uk Discount codes and vouchers for eating out, entertainment and more.

Books

www.abebooks.co.uk New and secondhand books, with special deals on textbooks.

www.alibris.co.uk New and secondhand books, movies and music.

www.amazon.co.uk New and secondhand books and more – and sell
your own unwanted goods too.

www.ebay.co.uk Buy (and sell) new and secondhand books at auction
or at a fixed price.

www.waterstones.co.uk The online home of this nationwide bookselling
chain.

Disability and dyslexia

www.skill.org.uk National bureau for students with disabilities.

www.bdadyslexia.org.uk Website for British Dyslexia Association.

www.nhs.uk/Conditions/Dyslexia/Pages/Introduction.aspx A short
introduction to dyslexia.

Emergencies and health

For police, ambulance and fire service emergencies, call 999.

For health information, call 0845 4647, 24 hours a day, or visit www.
nhsdirect.nhs.uk.

For information on healthy living, visit www.nhs.uk/livewell.

For mental health information, call 0300 123 3393, 9 am to 6 pm,
Monday to Friday, or visit www.mind.org.uk or www.rethink.org.

For mental health information in Scotland, visit www.seemescotland.org.
uk.

For information on drugs, call 0800 776600, 24 hours a day, or visit
www.talktofrank.com.

For confidential emotional support, call 08457 909090, 24 hours a day,
or visit www.samaritans.org.

General information for students

www.direct.gov.uk/en/EducationAndLearning/
UniversityAndHigherEducation From what higher education can do

for you to undergraduate information, this site has got the lot!

www.nus.org.uk The website of the National Union of Students.

www.thestudentroom.co.uk and www.studentsforum.co.uk Two
  lighthearted sites carrying information for students by students.

www.ucas.com Thinking of applying for another course or changed
  your mind about your current one? Check out UCAS for more
  information, a list of possible courses and useful contact numbers.

Getting a job

www.jobs.ac.uk A good site for jobs in education and for graduate jobs
  elsewhere.

www.jobsite.co.uk A job search site advertising jobs and giving careers
  advice, plus you can upload your CV to let employers search for you.

www.gumtree.com Job adverts – as well as free and cheap stuff!

www.reed.co.uk Another job search site advertising thousands of jobs in
  all sectors.

www.student-jobs.co.uk Full-time, part-time, summer and holiday jobs
  for students and graduates.

www.volunteering.org.uk An independent charity giving information
  about and support for volunteering.

7 Keys to a Winning CV: How to Create a CV That Gets Results by
  Mildred Talabi, published by Harriman House, available on Amazon
  and in all good bookshops. For more information, visit www.
  mildredtalabi.com/books.

Getting around

www.16–25railcard.co.uk Get an annual railcard and save money on
  your journeys.

www.megabus.com Low-cost tickets and information about coach
  travel.

www.nationalexpress.com Tickets and timetables for National Express
  coaches.

www.nationalrail.co.uk Rail travel news, train times and a cheapest fare finder.

www.tfl.gov.uk A journey planner for London and information about tube and bus services and tickets.

www.thetrainline.com Train times and tickets nationwide, and a best fare finder.

www.virgintrains.co.uk Tickets and information about Virgin Trains.

Help with assignments

www.apple.com/education Download lectures and talks, then listen to them on your iPhone or iPod.

www.coursework.info An online library of academic coursework, to which you can get access for a small fee or by publishing your own work on the site. The essays are submitted to Turnitin to prevent them being plagiarised.

www.skills4study.com Free study skills materials, including MP3 audio downloads.

International students

www.ukcisa.org.uk A website that protects and promotes the needs of international students.

www.internationalstudent.com This is a really good website that includes blogs, resources and loads of information.

www.educationuk.org Website for international students interested in a UK course or qualification.

Money matters

www.direct.gov.uk/en/EducationAndLearning/ UniversityAndHigherEducation/StudentFinance The best place for advice on how to apply for student finance, including a link to the Student Loans Company and appropriate forms.

www.slc.co.uk The website of the Student Loans Company.
www.comparethemarket.com A comparison site to find out the best
   prices for insurance, gas and electricity, credit cards and loans.
www.moneyaware.co.uk The website of the Consumer Credit
   Counselling Service, a charity that provides free debt and money-
   management advice.
www.moneysavingexpert.com Money advice and updates on deals,
   savings and new products.

Postgraduate study

www.postgrad.com Courses, information and news for postgraduates.
www.prospects.ac.uk Information on postgraduate courses and funding.

Travelling abroad

www.campamerica.co.uk Work as a counsellor or in the support team at
   summer camps in America.
www.esn.org The Erasmus Student Network, organising study abroad.
www.lonelyplanet.com Worldwide travel information.
www.statravel.co.uk Gap-year specialist travel agency.

Index